GoodFood
Easy student dinners

D0177151

10 9 8 7

Published in 2011 by BBC Books, an imprint of Ebury Publishing
A Random House Group company

Photographs © BBC Magazines 2011
Recipes © BBC Magazines 2011
Book design © Woodlands Books Ltd 2011
All recipes contained in this book first appeared in BBC *Good Food* magazine.

The Random House Group Limited
Reg. No. 954009

Addresses for companies within the Random House Group can be found at www.randomhouse.co.uk

A CIP catalogue record for this book is available from the British Library

The Random House Group Limited supports the Forest Stewardship Council® (FSC®), the leading international forest-certification organisation. Our books carrying the FSC label are printed on FSC®-certified paper. FSC is the only forest-certification scheme supported by the leading environmental organisations, including Greenpeace. Our paper procurement policy can be found at www.randomhouse.co.uk/environment

To buy books by your favourite authors and register for offers visit www.randomhouse.co.uk

Printed and bound by Firmengruppe APPL, aprinta druck, Wemding, Germany
Colour origination by Dot Gradations Ltd, UK

Commissioning Editor: Muna Reyal
Project Editor: Joe Cottington
Designer: Annette Peppis
Production: Rebecca Jones
Picture Researcher: Gabby Harrington

ISBN: 9781849902564

Picture credits

BBC *Good Food* magazine and BBC Books would like to thank the following people for providing photos. While every effort has been made to trace and acknowledge all photographers, we should like to apologise should there be any errors or omissions.

Iain Bagwell p97; Peter Cassidy p39, p143, p161, p197; Jean Cazals p25; Will Heap p57, p59, p61, p65, p69, p71, p73, p75, p77, p91, p103, p105, p133, p135, p167, p169, p171, p175, p177, p181, p185, p199, p201, p209, p211; Amanda Heywood p173, p191; Gareth Morgans p17, p23, p31, p41, p127, p155, p157, p159, p179, p189; David Munns p21, p51, p53, p83, p85, p89, p101, p129, p137, p139, p141, p165, p183, p187, p195, p207; Myles New p11, p35, p55, p79, p87, p107, p109, p119, p131, p145, p163; Maja Smend p19, p99; Brett Stevens p33; Roger Stowell p147; Lis Parsons p13, p15, p29, p43, p45, p47, p49, p63, p67, p81, p93, p113, p115, p117, p121, p123, p125, p149, p151, p153, p193, p203, p205; Simon Walton p37, p95, p111; Philip Webb p27

All the recipes in this book were created by the editorial team at *Good Food* and by regular contributors to BBC Magazines.

everyday GoodFood
Easy student dinners

Editor **Barney Desmazery**

Contents

Introduction

At *Good Food* we pride ourselves on the work we put into our recipes. For this book we've thought about all the challenges facing students – whether sharing the cooking with a group of friends or cooking for one. Every recipe is budget conscious and supermarket friendly, and has been triple-tested.

A good breakfast gives you the best start to the day, so we've given lots of options for more nutritious alternatives to a quick slice of toast. With a busy social life, time can often be an issue, so we've dedicated a chapter to recipes that are ready in half an hour or less; knowing that lots of student kitchens are a little sparse on cooking utensils, another chapter is full of recipes that can be made in just one dish.

Canny student cooking is all about clever housekeeping, so throughout each chapter we have given lots of options for recipes that can be batch-cooked and frozen so you can take full advantage of special food offers and get ahead on meals for another night.

Let's not forget the times for sharing – which is where the food for friends section comes in – and of course we've included something sweet to finish.

Just like us all, what students cook and eat has changed a lot over recent years, so we've made sure this collection of modern recipes hasn't compromised on flavour and proves that student food has come well beyond boil-in-the-bag in a bed-sit!

Barney Desmazery
Good Food magazine

Notes and conversion tables

NOTES ON THE RECIPES
• Eggs are large in the UK and Australia and extra large in America unless stated otherwise.
• Wash fresh produce before preparation.
• Recipes contain nutritional analyses for 'sugar', which means the total sugar content including all natural sugars in the ingredients, unless otherwise stated.

OVEN TEMPERATURES

Gas	°C	°C Fan	°F	Oven temp.
¼	110	90	225	Very cool
½	120	100	250	Very cool
1	140	120	275	Cool or slow
2	150	130	300	Cool or slow
3	160	140	325	Warm
4	180	160	350	Moderate
5	190	170	375	Moderately hot
6	200	180	400	Fairly hot
7	220	200	425	Hot
8	230	210	450	Very hot
9	240	220	475	Very hot

APPROXIMATE WEIGHT CONVERSIONS
• All the recipes in this book list both imperial and metric measurements. Conversions are approximate and have been rounded up or down. Follow one set of measurements only; do not mix the two.
• Cup measurements, which are used by cooks in Australia and America, have not been listed here as they vary from ingredient to ingredient. Kitchen scales should be used to measure dry/solid ingredients.

Good Food is concerned about sustainable sourcing and animal welfare. Where possible, humanely reared meats, sustainably caught fish (see fishonline.org for further information from the Marine Conservation Society) and free-range chickens and eggs are used when recipes are originally tested.

SPOON MEASURES

Spoon measurements are level unless otherwise specified.

• 1 teaspoon (tsp) = 5ml

• 1 tablespoon (tbsp) = 15ml

• 1 Australian tablespoon = 20ml (cooks in Australia should measure 3 teaspoons where 1 tablespoon is specified in a recipe)

APPROXIMATE LIQUID CONVERSIONS

metric	imperial	AUS	US
50ml	2fl oz	¼ cup	¼ cup
125ml	4fl oz	½ cup	½ cup
175ml	6fl oz	¾ cup	¾ cup
225ml	8fl oz	1 cup	1 cup
300ml	10fl oz/½ pint	½ pint	1¼ cups
450ml	16fl oz	2 cups	2 cups/1 pint
600ml	20fl oz/1 pint	1 pint	2½ cups
1 litre	35fl oz/1¾ pints	1¾ pints	1 quart

Blueberry Bircher pots

Avoid the lure of expensive pastries and takeaway coffee; these snacks help beat off the mid-morning munchies.

TAKES 10 MINUTES • MAKES 2

2 small apples
4 tbsp whole oats
4 tbsp low-fat natural yogurt
handful blueberries

1 Peel the apples and then, using the coarse side of a grater, grate the flesh until you get to the core.
2 In a bowl, mix the grated apple with the oats and yogurt. Layer the mixture into glasses, adding blueberries between the layers.

PER POT 124 kcals, protein 5g, carbs 24g, fat 2g, sat fat 0.4g, fibre 4g, sugar 14g, salt 0.07g

Spiced scrambled eggs

Make a wholesome start to the morning with creamy scrambled eggs on toast and also use up a stray tomato or two.

TAKES 30 MINUTES ● SERVES 2
knob of butter
1 small onion, chopped
1 red chilli, chopped
4 eggs, beaten
splash of milk
good handful diced tomatoes
sprinkling coriander leaves
buttered toast, to serve

1 Melt the butter in a pan until just starting to sizzle, then add the onion and chilli, and cook for about 8 minutes until softened. Stir in the beaten eggs and milk.
2 When nearly scrambled, gently stir in the diced tomatoes followed by some coriander leaves. Season and eat served on hot buttered toast.

PER SERVING 236 kcals, protein 16g, carbs 3g, fat 18g, sat fat 6g, fibre 1g, sugar 3g, salt 0.51g

Bacon & parsley hotcakes

Take care of your weekly cooking duties by making a batch of these cheesy hotcakes as a weekend brunch for your housemates.

TAKES 25 MINUTES • SERVES 4

100g/4oz smoked bacon, chopped
100g/4oz self-raising flour
50g/2oz grated mature Cheddar
1 tsp fresh thyme leaves or ½ tsp dried
2 tbsp chopped parsley leaves
2 eggs
6 tbsp milk
sunflower oil, for frying
4 poached eggs, to serve
crème fraîche and a thyme sprig,
    to garnish (optional)

1 Dry-fry the bacon until crisp and golden. Tip on to a plate to cool.
2 Mix the flour, cheese, herbs and bacon together in a bowl and season. Make a well in the centre and add the eggs. Beat with a wooden spoon, then gradually add the milk, drawing the flour into the centre. You should end up with a fairly thick batter.
3 Heat a little oil in a frying pan, drop in large spoonfuls of the batter, then cook until the hotcakes start to set around the edges. Flip them over, then cook until golden. Keep warm while you cook the remaining hotcakes.
4 Serve each person two hotcakes topped with a poached egg and a spoonful of crème fraîche, garnished with a thyme sprig, if they wish.

PER SERVING 201 kcals, protein 7g, carbs 10g, fat 15g, sat fat 4g, fibre none, sugar none, salt 0.68g

All-day breakfast

Take all the pan-juggling out of a cooked breakfast with this all-in-one remix and save on washing up too.

TAKES 35 MINUTES • SERVES 4

1 pack chipolata sausages
1 tbsp olive oil
8 rashers bacon
small punnet cherry tomatoes (about 250g/9oz)
2 tsp wholegrain mustard
4 eggs
toast, to serve

1 Heat oven to 220C/200C fan/gas 7. Toss the sausages and oil in a shallow roasting tin, then spread out in an even layer. Drape bacon rashers over the top and roast for 15–20 minutes until both are starting to brown and sizzle.
2 Move the bacon and sausages around so everything browns evenly. Scatter over the tomatoes and blob the mustard on to the sausages. Use a pair of tongs or a spoon to create four gaps for the eggs, then crack an egg into each gap. Put the tin back in the oven for around 5–8 minutes or until the egg whites are set and tomatoes are softening.

PER SERVING 587 kcals, protein 28g, carbs 13g, fat 48g, sat fat 15g, fibre 2g, sugar 5g, salt 3.67g

Dippy eggs with Marmite soldiers

Learn to cook the perfect soft-boiled egg and you'll never be short of a quick, hot breakfast option.

TAKES 10 MINUTES • SERVES 2

2 eggs
4 slices wholemeal bread
knob of butter, softened
Marmite, for spreading
mixed seeds, for dipping

1 Bring a pan of water to a simmer, add the eggs and cook for 2 minutes if they are at room temperature, 3 minutes if fridge-cold, then turn off the heat. Cover the pan and leave the eggs in the water for 2 minutes more.
2 Meanwhile, toast the wholemeal bread and spread each slice thinly with butter, then Marmite. To serve, cut the bread into soldiers and dip them into the soft-boiled eggs, then into a few mixed seeds set on the plate.

PER SERVING 372 kcals, protein 17g, carbs 31g, fat 21g, sat fat 8g, fibre 4g, sugar 2g, salt 1.09g

Vegan tomato & mushroom pancakes

Anyone would be happy with this filling vegan cooked breakfast, which is also good as a light lunch.

TAKES 25 MINUTES ● SERVES 2

140g/5oz white self-raising flour
400ml/14fl oz soya milk
vegetable oil, for frying

FOR THE TOPPING

2 tbsp vegetable oil
250g/9oz button mushrooms
250g/9oz pack cherry tomatoes, halved
2 tbsp soya cream or soya milk
large handful pine nuts
snipped chives, to garnish

1 Sift the flour and a pinch of salt into a blender. Add the soya milk and blend to make a smooth batter.

2 Heat a little oil in a medium non-stick frying pan until very hot. Pour about 3 tablespoons of the batter into the pan and cook over a medium heat until bubbles appear on the surface of the pancake. Flip the pancake over with a palette knife and cook the other side until golden brown. Repeat with the remaining batter, keeping the cooked pancakes warm as you go. You will make about eight.

3 For the topping, heat the oil in a frying pan. Cook the mushrooms until tender, add the tomatoes and cook for a couple of minutes. Pour in the soya cream or milk and pine nuts, then gently cook until combined. Divide the pancakes between two plates, then spoon over the tomatoes and mushrooms. Scatter with chives.

PER SERVING 609 kcals, protein 18g, carbs 59g, fat 35g, sat fat 4g, fibre 6g, sugar 6g, salt 0.87g

Honey-crunch granola with almonds & apricots

Vary the flavour of this high-fibre breakfast by adding whatever nuts, seeds and dried fruit you like.

TAKES 30 MINUTES • SERVES 6–8

200g/7oz clear honey
4 tbsp mild-flavoured oil, such as
    sunflower or rapeseed
300g/10oz rolled oats
100g/4oz whole unblanched almonds
1 tsp ground cinnamon
140g/5oz dried apricots, roughly
    chopped
yoghurt or milk and fresh fruit
    (optional), to serve

1 Heat oven to 180C/160C fan/gas 4. In a large pan, heat the honey and oil together until bubbling, then tip in the oats, almonds and cinnamon. Stir until the oats are well coated, then tip on to one or two large baking sheets, spreading the mixture out. Bake for 20–25 minutes until golden, stirring halfway through.

2 Remove from the oven and, while still hot, stir in the apricots. Spread out again and press down with a spatula to cool – this will help it to clump together. Once cool, serve with yogurt or milk, and fruit, if you like. The granola will keep in an airtight container for 3 weeks.

PER SERVING 497 kcals, protein 10g, carbs 70g, fat 21g, sat fat 3g, fibre 7g, sugar 37g, salt 0.06g

On-the-run breakfast bars

By making up a batch of these bars at the weekend and keeping them for the week you have a healthy breakfast option every day.

TAKES 40 MINUTES • MAKES 12

100g/4oz butter
3 tbsp golden syrup
85g/3oz demerara sugar
140g/5oz porridge oats
½ tsp ground cinnamon
50g/2oz desiccated coconut
2 tbsp linseeds, lightly crushed
1 tbsp sesame seeds
100g/4oz chopped hazelnuts

1 Heat oven to 160C/fan 140C/gas 3. Butter a 22cm-square baking tin. Melt the butter, syrup and sugar in a pan. Pour in the oats, cinnamon, coconut, seeds and nuts, mix, then pour into the tin. Bake for 30–35 minutes.

2 Leave to cool for 5 minutes then cut into slices. Will keep for 1 week in an airtight container.

PER BAR 245 kcals, protein 4g, carbs 20g, fat 17g, sat fat 7g, fibre 3g, sugar 11g, salt 0.16g

Open turkey BLT

Turkey is a cheaper alternative to chicken. For a spicy hit, sprinkle the steaks with Cajun seasoning before grilling.

TAKES 20 MINUTES ● SERVES 2

2 turkey steaks (about 140g/5oz each)
4 rashers smoked streaky bacon
2 slices Cheddar
½ loaf ciabatta, cut in half horizontally
2 tbsp mayonnaise
1 medium tomato, sliced
½ avocado, peeled, stoned and
   thinly sliced
4 lettuce leaves

1 Heat grill to high. Lay the turkey steaks and bacon on a large baking sheet and grill for 3 minutes on each side or until cooked through. Set the bacon aside and top the turkey steaks with the cheese slices. Put the ciabatta slices next to the turkey on the tray and return them both to the grill until the bread is toasted and the cheese melts.
2 Spread the toast with the mayonnaise and top with the cheesy turkey steaks, tomato, avocado, lettuce and bacon.

PER SERVING 685 kcals, protein 54g, carbs 42g, fat 35g, sat fat 9g, fibre 3g, sugar none, salt 3g

Sweetcorn & avocado wraps

If using fresh sweetcorn, stand it on one end and cut the kernels off with a sharp knife, using a downward motion.

TAKES 25 MINUTES • SERVES 4

350g/12oz fresh or frozen sweetcorn kernels (stripped from about 4 cobs)
½ tsp cumin seeds
2 large ripe avocados, halved, stoned and peeled
juice 1 lime
2 large red chillies, deseeded and finely chopped
4 spring onions, finely sliced
14 basil leaves, finely shredded
½ tsp caster sugar
4 large flour tortilla wraps
50g bag rocket or other salad leaves

1 Bring a medium pan of water to the boil and add the sweetcorn. Return to the boil and simmer for 2 minutes, then drain in a colander. Refresh under cold running water, then leave to drain thoroughly. Heat a small frying pan, add the cumin seeds and toast for 1 minute until fragrant. Remove from the pan and cool.

2 Mash the avocado with a fork in a bowl leaving it a little lumpy, then stir in the lime juice, sweetcorn, cumin, chillies, spring onions, basil, sugar and some seasoning. To assemble, lay a wrap on a flat board and put a quarter of the avocado mix near the bottom, leaving a border. Top with a quarter of the rocket, then fold over the sides of the wrap, roll up and tuck in the edges to make a parcel. Repeat with the rest. Cut all the wraps in half to serve.

PER SERVING 446 kcals, protein 10g, carbs 47g, fat 25g, sat fat 3g, fibre 6g, sugar 4g, salt 0.58g

Toaster pitta pocket

If you're famished and can't wait for your next meal, this clever toastie will keep you going. Make as many as you need to tide you over!

TAKES 10 MINUTES • MAKES 1

1 mini pitta bread
1 tbsp soft cheese
1 tbsp grated Cheddar
your favourite fillings – ham, tomatoes, sweetcorn, ready-roasted peppers from a jar and tuna are good

1 Pop the pitta into the toaster for 30 seconds–1 minute, until just puffed but not crisp.
2 Meanwhile, mix together the cheeses. Slice an opening at one end of the pitta and use a teaspoon or a knife to spread the cheese mixture in. Push in some of your favourite fillings, gently squash the pitta closed between your hands, then put back in the toaster – cut-side up. Toast for 1–2 minutes until nicely golden and crisp.

PER TOASTIE (with ham & tomatoes) 333 kcals, protein 15g, carbs 43g, fat 13g, sat fat 7g, fibre 2g, sugar 4g, salt 1.91g

Salsa chicken & cheese tortillas

Packs of tortillas have quite a decent shelf life, so they're especially useful if you've run out of bread.

TAKES 15 MINUTES • SERVES 2

4 tbsp hot salsa from a jar
2 large flour tortillas, seeded or plain
215g can kidney beans, drained and
    roughly mashed
1 spring onion, chopped
50g/2oz leftover roast chicken,
    shredded
85g/3oz grated mature Cheddar
½ × 20g pack coriander, leaves
    chopped (optional)
oil, for brushing
lime wedges and coriander sprigs,
    to garnish

1 Spread 2 tablespoons of the salsa on to each tortilla, then evenly top one of them with the beans, spring onion, chicken and Cheddar. Scatter with coriander, if you have it. Sandwich with the other tortilla, then brush the top surface with oil.
2 Heat a large non-stick frying pan, then cook the tortilla, oil-side down, for 4 minutes. Carefully turn over with a palette knife (or by turning it out on to a plate, then sliding it back into the pan), then cook for 2 minutes on the other side until golden. Serve cut into wedges, sprinkled with the coriander and with a lime wedge on the side.

PER SERVING 533 kcals, protein 27g, carbs 44g, fat 29g, sat fat 12g, fibre 6g, sugar 7g, salt 3.18g

Nutty apple sarnie

One for the lunchbox, this healthy high-fibre sandwich will see you through to dinnertime.

TAKES 5 MINUTES • MAKES 1

small handful watercress
1 small apple
2 tbsp crunchy peanut butter
1 small wholegrain roll

1 Wash and dry the watercress, if it needs it, and quarter, core and thinly slice the apple. Spread the crunchy peanut butter over the wholegrain roll and top with the sliced apple and the watercress. Eat straight away or pack away in a lunchbox.

PER SERVING 345 kcals, protein 14g, carbs 35g, fat 18g, sat fat 4g, fibre 6g, sugar 6g, salt 0.96g

Vegetarian club

Deep-filled and piled high, this substantial sandwich has the bonus of being satisfying and superhealthy.

TAKES 10 MINUTES ● MAKES 1

3 slices granary bread
large handful watercress
1 carrot, peeled and coarsely grated
small squeeze lemon juice
1 tbsp olive oil
2 tbsp reduced-fat houmous
2 tomatoes, thickly sliced

1 Toast the bread. Meanwhile, mix the watercress, carrot, lemon juice and olive oil together in a small bowl.

2 Spread the houmous over each slice of toast. Top one slice with the watercress and carrot salad and a few slices of tomato, then sandwich with another slice of toast and top with more tomato. Lay the final slice of bread, houmous-side down, then press down and eat as is or cut the sandwich into quarters.

PER SERVING 299 kcals, protein 11g, carbs 50g, fat 7g, sat fat 1g, fibre 7g, sugar 15g, salt 1.50g

Tangy couscous salad

This veggie salad is great for grazing on as it will keep happily in the fridge for a couple of days.

TAKES 15 MINUTES • SERVES 4
300g/10oz couscous or bulghar wheat
vegetable stock
2 courgettes
1 tbsp olive oil
100g/4oz feta, crumbled
20g pack flat-leaf parsley, chopped
juice 1 lemon

1 Cook the couscous or bulghar wheat in vegetable stock according to the pack instructions. Trim the ends off the courgettes, then cut into slices.
2 Heat a griddle pan or grill. Drizzle the courgette slices with oil, then season. Cook for 2 minutes, then turn over and cook 1–2 minutes more until softened and golden brown. Tip into a large bowl along with the cooked couscous or bulghar wheat, then mix through the remaining ingredients. Best served at room temperature.

PER SERVING 269 kcals, protein 9g, carbs none, fat 9g, sat fat 4g, fibre 1g, sugar 3g, salt 0.92g

Healthy coleslaw

Using a mix of yogurt with mayonnaise in coleslaw gives it a nice tang and makes it healthier.

TAKES 10 MINUTES • SERVES 6

6 tbsp plain yogurt
½ tsp Dijon mustard
2 tbsp mayonnaise
½ white cabbage
2 carrots
½ onion

1 Mix the yogurt, mustard and mayonnaise together in a bowl. Using a grater attachment on a food processor or a box grater, coarsely grate the cabbage and carrots. Either grate the onion or chop it as finely as you can.

2 Tip all of the vegetables into the bowl and stir through the dressing. Will keep in the fridge for up to 3 days.

PER SERVING 76 kcals, protein 2g, carbs 8g, fat 4g, sat fat 1g, fibre 2g, sugar 7g, salt 0.15g

One-pot chicken pilaf

An ideal hassle-free supper with hardly any washing up. There are no scales required, just use a normal-size mug to measure out the ingredients.

TAKES 25 MINUTES • SERVES 1

1 tsp sunflower oil
1 small onion, chopped
1 large or 2 small skinless chicken thigh
    fillets, cut into chunks
2 tsp curry paste (choose your
    favourite)
⅓ mug basmati rice
⅔ mug chicken stock
1 mug frozen mixed veg
½ mug frozen leaf spinach

1 Heat the oil in a frying pan, then fry the onion for 5–6 minutes until softened. Add the chicken pieces, fry for a further couple of minutes, just to colour the outside, then stir in curry paste and rice. Cook for another minute.

2 Pour in the chicken stock and throw in any larger bits of frozen mixed veg. Bring to the boil, lower the heat, then cover the pan with a lid. Cook for 10 minutes, then stir in the remaining veg. Scatter over the spinach, cover, then cook for 10 minutes more until all the stock is absorbed and the rice is tender. Give everything a good stir, season to taste, then tuck in.

PER SERVING 663 kcals, protein 50g, carbs 92g, fat 13g, sat fat 2g, fibre 10g, sugar 13g, salt 1.94g

Gnocchi with lemon & chive pesto

To increase the veg count, cook some small broccoli florets, green beans or peas with the gnocchi.

TAKES 15 MINUTES ● SERVES 2

1 garlic clove, finely chopped
small bunch parsley, finely chopped
small bunch chives, snipped
2 tbsp toasted pine nuts, roughly
    chopped
2 tbsp grated Parmesan, or vegetarian
    alternative, plus extra for sprinkling
    (optional)
zest and juice 1 lemon
4 tbsp olive oil
500g pack gnocchi

1 Put the garlic, herbs, pine nuts, cheese and lemon zest in a small bowl, season well, then stir in the olive oil and lemon juice. Set aside.

2 Cook the gnocchi in a pan of salted boiling water, following the pack instructions, then drain well. Tip into a serving bowl and toss through the pesto. Serve with extra grated Parmesan, if you like.

PER SERVING 667 kcals, protein 15g, carbs 85g, fat 32g, sat fat 6g, fibre 4g, sugar 5g, salt 2.7g

Spicy mushroom & broccoli noodles

Easy to shop for and on the table in less than half an hour, which makes this a great weeknight veggie treat for two.

TAKES 20 MINUTES • SERVES 2

1 low-salt vegetable stock cube
2 nests medium egg noodles
1 small head broccoli, broken into florets
1 tbsp sesame oil, plus extra to taste (optional)
250g pack shiitake or chestnut mushrooms, thickly sliced
1 fat garlic clove, finely chopped
½ tsp chilli flakes
4 spring onions, thinly sliced
2 tbsp hoisin sauce
handful roasted cashew nuts

1 Put the stock cube into a pan of water, then bring to the boil. Add the noodles, bring the stock back to the boil and cook for 2 minutes. Add the broccoli and boil for 2 minutes more. Reserve a cup of the stock, then drain the noodles and veg.

2 Heat a frying pan or wok, add the sesame oil and stir-fry the mushrooms for 2 minutes until turning golden. Add the garlic, chilli flakes and most of the spring onions, cook for 1 minute more, then tip in the noodles and broccoli. Splash in 3 tablespoons of the reserved stock and the hoisin sauce, then toss together for 1 minute using a pair of tongs or two wooden spoons.

3 Serve the noodles scattered with the cashew nuts and remaining spring onions. Add a dash more sesame oil to taste, if you like.

PER SERVING 624 kcals, protein 25g, carbs 105g, fat 14g, sat fat 2g, fibre 8g, sugar 17g, salt 2.35g

Ham, pesto & fish bake

Prosciutto gives this recipe an Italian twist, but if it's too expensive you can use thinly sliced bacon instead.

TAKES 20 MINUTES • SERVES 4

4 chunky white fish fillets
4 slices prosciutto
200g pot crème fraîche
3 tbsp basil pesto
25g/1oz Parmesan, finely grated
1 tbsp pine nuts
good crusty bread, to serve

1 Heat oven to 200C/180C fan/gas 6. Season the fish all over, then wrap each fillet in a slice of ham. Put into a large baking dish. Dot the crème fraîche among the fillets and over the exposed ends of the fish. Dot the pesto around the fish, too. Scatter with the cheese.

2 Bake the fish for 15–20 minutes, adding the pine nuts halfway through, until the crème fraîche has made a sauce around the fish, and the cheese and ham are turning golden. Serve with plenty of crusty bread to mop up the extra sauce.

PER SERVING 406 kcals, protein 34g, carbs 2g, fat 29g, sat fat 16g, fibre none, sugar 1g, salt 0.82g

Noodles with turkey, green beans & hoisin

Hoisin sauce is a good storecupboard stand-by to add heaps of authentic oriental flavour to any stir-fry.

TAKES 25 MINUTES ● SERVES 2

100g/4oz ramen noodles
100g/4oz green beans, halved
3 tbsp hoisin sauce
juice 1 lime
1 tbsp chilli sauce
1 tbsp vegetable oil
250g/9oz minced turkey
2 garlic cloves, chopped
6 spring onions, sliced diagonally

1 Boil the noodles, following the pack instructions, adding the green beans for the final 2 minutes. Drain and set aside.

2 In a small bowl, mix together the hoisin, lime juice and chilli sauce. In a wok or frying pan, heat the oil, then fry the mince until nicely browned. Add the garlic and fry for 1 minute more. Stir in the hoisin mixture and cook for a few minutes more until sticky. Finally, stir in the noodles, beans and half the spring onions to heat through. Scatter over the remaining spring onions to garnish and serve.

PER SERVING 415 kcals, protein 36g, carbs 50g, fat 9g, sat fat 1g, fibre 4g, sugar 11g, salt 2.3g

Sausage & broccoli pasta

Sausages that contain flavours like sun-dried tomatoes, caramelised onions, Parmesan or fennel work well in this dish.

TAKES 25 MINUTES ● SERVES 2

200g/7oz pasta shapes

150g pack purple sprouting broccoli, cut into pieces

2 tbsp extra virgin olive oil

2 garlic cloves, sliced

½ tsp fennel seeds (optional)

½ tsp crushed red chillies

2 Italian-style pork sausages, skins removed and meat broken into pieces

Parmesan shavings, to garnish

1 Bring a large pan of water to the boil and cook the pasta until nearly al dente. Throw in the broccoli and cook for around 2 minutes more. Drain, saving 1–2 tablespoons of the water.

2 Heat the oil in a large frying pan and add the garlic, fennel seeds, if using, and chillies. When they start to colour a bit, add the sausage and cook until golden and cooked through. Tip in the drained pasta and broccoli with the reserved water and toss. Serve hot with the Parmesan shavings scattered over.

PER SERVING 738 kcals, protein 34g, carbs 80g, fat 34g, sat fat 11g, fibre 7g, sugar 5g, salt 1.25g

Prawn & pea korma

This is a mild curry, but if you prefer a bit more heat, swap the korma paste for something hotter.

TAKES 25 MINUTES ● SERVES 4

1 tbsp vegetable oil
2 onions, thinly sliced
3 tbsp korma paste
1 cinnamon stick
400ml/14fl oz vegetable or
    chicken stock
200g/7oz basmati rice, rinsed
200g/7oz frozen peas
200g/7oz cooked frozen prawns,
    defrosted
200g/7oz Greek yogurt
50g/2oz ground almonds
½ small pack coriander leaves,
    chopped, to garnish

1 Heat the vegetable oil in a large frying pan with the onions and soften for 10 minutes. Add the korma paste and cinnamon, and fry for 3 minutes more. Pour in the stock and simmer for another 3 minutes.

2 Meanwhile, cook the basmati rice following the pack instructions.

3 Tip the peas and prawns into the korma sauce and gently cook until piping hot. Stir in the Greek yogurt, almonds and seasoning. Discard the cinnamon, scatter the curry with coriander and serve with the rice.

PER SERVING 463 kcals, protein 25g, carbs 53g, fat 18g, sat fat 4g, fibre 5g, sugar 7g, salt 2.44g

Bolognese bake

If you like lasagne you will love this pasta bake, which has all of the same flavours but is quicker and easier.

TAKES 25 MINUTES ● SERVES 6

400g lean minced beef
3 garlic cloves, crushed
1 tbsp caster sugar
1 tbsp dried mixed herbs
690ml jar passata with onions and
    garlic
350g/12oz penne
200ml tub half-fat crème fraîche
25g/1oz Parmesan, grated
green salad, to serve

1 In a large, non-stick frying pan, dry-fry the mince until browned. Add the garlic, sugar and herbs, and cook for 1 minute more. Pour over the passata, add some seasoning, then simmer while you cook the pasta following the pack instructions.
2 Meanwhile, combine the crème fraîche and Parmesan. Heat grill to high. Spoon half the mince into an ovenproof dish. Mix the rest with the pasta and pour this on top. Drizzle over the Parmesan cream and grill until golden and bubbling. Serve with salad.

PER SERVING 449 kcals, protein 25g, carbs 54g, fat 15g, sat fat 7g, fibre 2g, sugar 9g, salt 0.85g

Spaghetti with walnuts, raisins & parsley

This out-of-the ordinary vegetarian pasta dish couldn't be any easier to make.

TAKES 20 MINUTES • SERVES 4

300g/10oz spaghetti
2 tbsp olive oil
2 onions, sliced
5 tbsp raisins or sultanas
250ml/9fl oz vegetable stock
50g/2oz Parmesan, grated
5 tbsp chopped walnuts
small bunch flat-leaf parsley, finely
    chopped

1 Cook the pasta in boiling water, following the pack instructions. Drain.
2 Meanwhile, heat the oil in a frying pan and cook the onions until soft and golden brown – about 8–10 minutes. Add the raisins or sultanas and stock, and cook for 2–3 minutes until hot through. Toss with the pasta, Parmesan, walnuts and parsley.

PER SERVING 526 kcals, protein 18g, carbs 74g, fat 19g, sat fat 4g, fibre 4g, sugar 19g, salt 0.44g

Spicy vegetable egg-fried rice

Mix it up with different veg in your fried rice – broccoli, bok choi, baby corn and mangetout are all great additions.

TAKES 25 MINUTES • SERVES 4

200g/7oz basmati rice or 400g/14oz leftover cooked rice

1–2 red chillies, deseeded and grated or very finely chopped

3 garlic cloves, crushed

1 tbsp sunflower oil

2 large carrots, diced

200g/7oz Chinese cabbage, finely sliced

2 eggs, lightly beaten

3 spring onions, sliced

200g/7oz frozen peas

1 tbsp soy sauce, plus extra to taste (optional)

1 If making the rice from scratch, cook it following the pack instructions, then drain. Mix the chillies and garlic (in a pestle and mortar, if you have one) with a pinch of salt to make a paste.

2 Heat the oil in a wok or large frying pan on a medium–high heat. Add the carrots and stir-fry for 5 minutes until tender. Add the cabbage and chilli paste, and cook for 1 minute more. Tip in the cooked basmati or leftover rice and stir-fry for 1 minute until piping hot.

3 Push the rice mixture to one side of the pan. Add the eggs to the cleared space and scramble until set. Mix in the onions, peas and soy sauce, and stir-fry everything together until the peas are hot. Serve with extra soy sauce to taste.

PER SERVING 305 kcals, protein 12g, carbs 52g, fat 7g, sat fat 2g, fibre 6g, sugar 8g, salt 0.84g

Tex-Mex beef tacos

Just mix-and-match your favourite taco toppings with this sauce. Shredded lettuce, grated cheese and chopped tomato all work well.

TAKES 25 MINUTES • SERVES 6

500g pack lean minced beef
1 tbsp sunflower oil
4 garlic cloves, crushed
1½ tbsp dried oregano
2 tsp ground cumin
2 tsp paprika
pinch chilli flakes
24 taco shells
soured cream and grated Cheddar,
   to garnish

1 Heat a large frying pan until very hot, then brown the mince. Remove, then season with salt and pepper. Add the oil to the pan and fry the garlic, oregano and spices for 1 minute until fragrant. Return the beef to the pan and toss well, then cook for 2–3 minutes until hot all the way through.

2 Warm the taco shells following the pack instructions and serve with the beef, topped with soured cream and some grated Cheddar.

PER SERVING 383 kcals, protein 22g, carbs 29g, fat 21g, sat fat 4g, fibre 2g, sugar 1g, salt 1.17g

Halloumi with couscous & chickpea salsa

An easy modern vegetarian supper that's smart enough to serve at a special gathering.

TAKES 20 MINUTES • SERVES 4

250g/9oz couscous
250ml/9fl oz hot vegetable stock
400g tin chickpeas, drained and rinsed
140g/5oz cherry tomatoes, halved
3 tbsp olive oil, plus extra for frying
3 tbsp red wine vinegar
1 red chilli, ½ deseeded and finely
    chopped, ½ sliced
small bunch each mint and coriander
    leaves, chopped
250g pack halloumi cheese, thickly
    sliced

1 Put the couscous in a bowl and pour over the hot stock. Cover with cling film and leave to stand and swell for 10 minutes.

2 Make the salsa by mixing the chickpeas with the tomatoes, half the oil and vinegar, the finely chopped chillies and some of the chopped herbs. Season and arrange among four serving plates.

3 Heat a little oil in a griddle or frying pan and fry the halloumi for 2–3 minutes each side until golden and lightly charred.

4 Fluff up the couscous with a fork and mix in the rest of the oil, vinegar and herbs with some seasoning. Pile on to the plates next to the salsa and top with the warm halloumi. Garnish with the sliced chillies.

PER SERVING 498 kcals, protein 21g, carbs 44g, fat 28g, sat fat 11g, fibre 3g, sugar 3g, salt 2.79g

Chicken Caesar salad

This recipe proves there is nothing tricky about making this classic main-meal salad.

TAKES 25 MINUTES • SERVES 4

4 thick slices crusty white bread, roughly chopped into chunky croutons
3 tbsp olive oil
2 boneless skinless chicken breasts
1 large cos or romaine lettuce leaves, separated

FOR THE DRESSING

1 garlic clove
2 anchovies, from a tin
small block Parmesan or Grana Padano, for grating and shaving
5 tbsp mayonnaise
1 tbsp white wine vinegar

1 Heat oven to 200C/180C fan/gas 6. Spread the croutons over a baking sheet and drizzle over 2 tablespoons of the olive oil. Bake for 8–10 minutes, turning once in a while.

2 Rub the chicken breasts with the remaining oil and season. Heat a griddle pan and cook the chicken for 4 minutes on both sides, or until cooked. Set aside.

3 Crush the garlic and mash the anchovies. Grate a handful of cheese and mix with the rest of the dressing ingredients. Season to taste. It should be the consistency of yogurt – if it is thicker, stir in a few teaspoons of water to thin it.

4 Shave the rest of the cheese with a peeler. Tear the lettuce into large pieces in a large bowl. Shred the chicken into bite-sized strips and scatter half over the leaves, along with half the croutons. Add most of the dressing and toss with your fingers. Scatter over the rest of the chicken and croutons, then drizzle with the remaining dressing. Sprinkle the cheese shavings on top and serve.

PER SERVING 461 kcals, protein 27g, carbs 28g, fat 28g, sat fat 6g, fibre 2g, sugar 4g, salt 1.39g

Indian minced lamb skewers

Cheap but packed with flavour, this recipe takes hardly any time and can be easily doubled if feeding a crowd.

TAKES 25 MINUTES ● **SERVES 4**

500g pack minced lamb
1 onion, finely chopped
3 tbsp curry paste
small bunch coriander leaves,
    roughly chopped
2 naan breads
120g bag herb salad
200g tub raita

1 Heat oven to 220C/200C fan/gas 7. In a medium bowl, combine the lamb, onion, curry paste and most of the coriander with some seasoning. Press 2–3 tablespoons of the lamb around skewers to form kebabs and transfer to a baking sheet.

2 Cook for 15–20 minutes until golden and cooked through. Warm the naan breads, following the pack instructions. Serve the kebabs with the herb salad , naan bread and raita to dollop over.

PER SERVING 542 kcals, protein 31g, carbs 36g, fat 31g, sat fat 15g, fibre 3g, sugar 6g, salt 1.83g

Creamy seafood stew

Take the frozen seafood out of the freezer and defrost it in the fridge overnight so it is ready to use when you start cooking

TAKES 25 MINUTES ● SERVES 3

1 tbsp olive oil
1 onion, chopped
2 celery sticks, chopped
1 garlic clove, crushed
175ml/6fl oz white wine
300ml/½ pint chicken stock
1 tbsp cornflour, mixed with 1 tbsp
   cold water
75ml/2½fl oz double cream
400g bag frozen mixed seafood,
   defrosted
small bunch dill leaves, chopped
garlic bread, to serve

1 Heat the oil in a large frying pan and cook the onion and celery until soft but not coloured, about 10 minutes. Throw in the garlic and cook for 1 minute more. Pour in the wine and simmer on a high heat until most of it has disappeared.

2 Pour in the stock, cornflour mix and the cream, and simmer for 5–10 minutes, stirring often until thickened. Season and then add the seafood and most of the dill. Simmer for a few minutes until piping hot.

3 Cook the garlic bread, following the pack instructions, and divide the stew into warm bowls, scattered with the remaining dill. Serve with garlic bread for dipping into the sauce.

PER SERVING 324 kcals, protein 24g, carbs 10g, fat 19g, sat fat 8g, fibre 1g, sugar 6g, salt 1.34g

Full-English carbonara

If it's your turn to cook, this filling pasta dish is full of familiar flavours that all your friends are bound to love.

TAKES 25 MINUTES • SERVES 4

4 sausages, skins removed and meat
   squeezed out
4 rashers bacon, diced
200g/7oz mushrooms, chopped
350g/12oz pasta shapes
50g/2oz Parmesan, grated, plus extra
   to sprinkle
2 egg yolks
small bunch flat-leaf parsley, finely
   chopped
100ml/3½fl oz double cream

1 Dry-fry the sausage meat in a non-stick pan for 8–10 minutes until browned, breaking it up with a wooden spoon. Remove and set aside. Fry the bacon and mushrooms for 5–8 minutes until golden, return the sausage meat to the pan and keep warm.

2 Cook the pasta, following the pack instructions. Meanwhile, make the sauce by beating together the Parmesan, egg yolks, most of the parsley and the cream. When the pasta is cooked, drain, reserving half a cupful of the cooking water for use later on.

3 Combine the pasta and meat mixture on the hob with the heat turned off, then add the sauce. Season and mix well, adding a splash of cooking water if it's a little thick. Spoon into bowls and eat with extra Parmesan cheese and the remaining parsley sprinkled on top.

PER SERVING 753 kcals, protein 28g, carbs 73g, fat 41g, sat fat 18g, fibre 4g, sugar 4g, salt 1.97g

Chicken parmigiana

Stretch a packet of two chicken breasts to serve four by giving them a filling, crispy coating.

TAKES 30 MINUTES ● SERVES 4

2 large boneless skinless chicken
   breasts, halved through the middle
2 eggs, beaten
85g/3oz breadcrumbs
85g/3oz Parmesan, grated
1 tbsp olive oil
2 garlic cloves, crushed
½ jar passata
1 tsp caster sugar
1 tsp oregano
½ × 125g ball mozzarella, torn
cooked spaghetti, to serve (optional)

1 Put the chicken breasts between sheets of cling film and bash out with a rolling pin until the thickness of a £1 coin. Dip in the egg and then dredge in the breadcrumbs and half the Parmesan. Set aside on a plate in the fridge to rest.

2 To make the tomato sauce, heat the oil and cook the garlic for 1 minute, then tip in the passata, sugar, oregano and some salt and pepper, and simmer for 5–10 minutes.

3 Heat grill to high and cook the chicken for 5 minutes each side, then remove. Pour the tomato sauce into a shallow ovenproof dish and top with the chicken. Scatter over the mozzarella and remaining Parmesan and grill for 3–4 minutes until the cheese has melted and the sauce is bubbling. Serve with spaghetti, if you like.

PER SERVING 378 kcals, protein 38g, carbs 21g, fat 16g, sat fat 7g, fibre 1g, sugar 5g, salt 1.56g

Salmon & soft cheese baked potato

For a quicker option, prick a potato with a fork, wrap it in a sheet of kitchen paper and microwave on High for 8–10 minutes until soft inside.

TAKES 1¼ HOURS • SERVES 1

sunflower oil, for greasing
1 baking potato
50g/2oz light soft cheese
a little lemon zest and a squeeze
    lemon juice
1 hot-smoked salmon fillet
1 heaped tsp capers

1 Heat oven to 220C/200C fan/gas 7. Rub a little oil and seasoning over the potato, then bake on a baking sheet for 25 minutes. Turn down the oven to 190C/170C fan/gas 5 and bake for 1–1¼ hours more until the flesh is tender and the skin is crisp and golden.
2 While the potato is baking, make the filling. Mix the soft cheese with the lemon juice and some seasoning.
3 To serve, slice a cross in the centre of the potato and squeeze the base to 'pop' the top. Pile the soft cheese filling into the potato and flake the salmon fillet on top. Sprinkle with the capers and a little of the lemon zest.

PER SERVING 580 kcals, protein 29g, carbs 60g, fat 27g, sat fat 9g, fibre 5g, sugar 4g, salt 3g

Mussels in red pesto

Mussels may sound restauranty but they are actually cheap, quick, easy, healthy and great for a solo supper.

TAKES 15 MINUTES • SERVES 1

1 tsp olive oil
1 shallot, finely chopped
1 small glass white wine or water
pinch crushed chilli flakes
500g/1lb 2oz clean live mussels
2 tbsp red pesto
crusty bread, to serve

1 Heat the oil in a large pan and cook the shallot for 4–5 minutes until softened. Pour in the wine or water, add the chilli flakes and bubble for 2 minutes.

2 Add the mussels. Cover and cook for 5 minutes until all the shells have opened. Discard any that remain closed. Stir in the red pesto and toss well. Tip into a large bowl and serve with some crusty bread.

PER SERVING (without bread) 311 kcals, protein 25g, carbs 11g, fat 15g, sat fat 3g, fibre none, sugar 6g, salt 1.49g

Croque madame with spinach salad

This bistro classic takes the ham and cheese toastie to a whole new level.

TAKES 15 MINUTES • SERVES 1

1 thick slice crusty white bread
1½ tsp wholegrain or Dijon mustard
2 thin slices ham, trimmed of fat
50g/2oz mature Cheddar or other
    melting cheese, grated
½ tsp cider vinegar or white wine
    vinegar
1 tsp mild olive oil, plus a little for
    frying
1 egg
handful baby leaf spinach from
    100g bag

1 Heat grill to high and lightly toast the bread on both sides. Spread 1 teaspoon of the mustard over one side, then top with the ham and cheese. Whisk the remaining mustard and vinegar with the oil and some seasoning. Grill the croque for 3 minutes, or until the cheese is bubbling and turning golden.

2 Meanwhile, heat a non-stick frying pan, add a little oil, then crack in the egg and gently fry to your liking. When cooked, set it on top of the croque on a plate. Toss the dressing with the spinach then serve with the croque and eat straight away.

PER SERVING 504 kcals, protein 32g, carbs 22g, fat 33g, sat fat 14g, fibre 2g, sugar 3g, salt 3.1g

Quick prawn noodle soup

To make this soup Japanese, swap the fish sauce, lime juice, star anise and sugar for a sachet of miso soup or 1 tablespoon miso paste.

TAKES 15 MINUTES • SERVES 1

85g/3oz thick rice noodles

500ml/18fl oz hot chicken or vegetable stock

1 tsp fish sauce

juice ½ lime

1 star anise

pinch sugar

handful small raw prawns

handful mint and coriander leaves and some chopped and deseeded red chilli, to serve

1 Boil the noodles following the pack instructions until just cooked, then drain.

2 Put the stock in a pan with the fish sauce, lime juice, star anise and sugar. Bring to the boil and add the noodles and prawns. Warm through, then pour into a bowl and serve topped with the mint, coriander and chilli.

PER SERVING 256 kcals, protein 31g, carbs 30g, fat 3g, sat fat none, fibre 2g, sugar 3g, salt 3.33g

Flattened chicken with tomatoes, olives & capers

This summery one-pan supper needs nothing more than some steamed potatoes to mop up the delicious juices.

TAKES 20 MINUTES ● SERVES 1

1 boneless skinless chicken breast
a little seasoned flour, for dusting
1 tbsp olive oil
1 large ripe tomato, chopped
2 tsp capers
handful pitted olives
splash white wine (or water, if you prefer)
snipped chives or chopped parsley, to garnish

1 Split the chicken breast almost in half and open it out like a book. Bash with a rolling pin to flatten, then lightly coat in the seasoned flour. Heat the oil in a pan, add the chicken and cook for 3–4 minutes on each side until crisp, browned and cooked through. Remove from the pan and keep warm.

2 Add the tomato, capers, olives and wine (or water) to the pan, season to taste, then bring to the boil. Bubble the sauce for 2–3 minutes until the tomatoes are starting to break down, then spoon over the chicken and scatter with chopped herbs before serving.

PER SERVING 339 kcals, protein 36g, carbs 9g, fat 17g, sat fat 3g, fibre 3g, sugar 5g, salt 2.78g

Pork with garlicky bean mash

Use the rest of the can of beans from this recipe to make a single serving of salad the next day.

TAKES 20 MINUTES • SERVES 1

1 pork steak, trimmed of fat
1 tbsp olive oil
1 small onion or shallot, chopped
1 garlic clove, crushed
½ × 410g can haricot beans in water,
  drained and rinsed
125ml/4fl oz vegetable stock
1 tbsp chopped coriander leaves

1 Grill the pork for 12–15 minutes, turning once until browned and completely cooked through.

2 Heat the oil in a small pan, add the onion or shallot and fry for 3 minutes until softened. Add the garlic, fry for 1 minute more, then tip in the beans and stock, and simmer for 5 minutes. Roughly mash with a potato masher or fork, then stir in the coriander. Serve with the pork.

PER SERVING 444 kcals, protein 42g, carbs 30g, fat 18g, sat fat 3g, fibre 9g, sugar 7g, salt 0.39g

Treat yourself steak supper

Steak is ideal for one: it's so quick and easy. For a clever, simple accompaniment, try this cheats' Béarnaise sauce.

TAKES 30 MINUTES • SERVES 1

2 tbsp vegetable oil
1 medium potato, peeled and cut into small chunks
200g/7oz beef steak (rump or sirloin, if you can afford it)
1 tbsp red wine vinegar
2 tbsp crème fraîche
1 tbsp wholegrain mustard
1 tbsp chopped fresh tarragon
green salad, to serve

1 Heat 1 tablespoon of the oil in a small non-stick frying pan with a lid. Tip the potato into the pan, cover, and cook for 10 minutes, shaking the pan occasionally so the potatoes get tossed around. Remove the lid and fry the potato, uncovered, for another 4–5 minutes, until crisp and golden.

2 Meanwhile, season the steak. About 5 minutes before the potatoes are ready, heat the remaining oil in a small heavy-based frying pan and fry the steak for 1½–2 minutes on each side, depending how you like it done.

3 Take the steak out of the pan and put it on a warmed plate. Turn down the heat, spoon in the vinegar (it will evaporate immediately), then quickly stir in the crème fraîche and mustard, and heat just until they melt and make a sauce. Sprinkle in most of the tarragon, stir and taste for seasoning. Pour the sauce over the steak and scatter with the remaining tarragon. Serve with the crisp potatoes and a green salad.

PER SERVING 681 kcals, protein 52g, carbs 24g, fat 42 g, sat fat 11g, fibre 2.4g, salt 1.1 g

Sizzled lamb chops & courgettes

Griddling the lamb and courgettes gives you the flavour of a barbecue without all the effort of cooking outdoors.

TAKES 15 MINUTES ● SERVES 1

zest and juice 1 lemon
1 tbsp olive oil
pinch dried thyme
3 lamb chops
1 courgette, thickly sliced on the
    diagonal
2 tbsp houmous (optional)

1 Mix the lemon zest and juice, oil and thyme in a small bowl, then pour half over the chops. Set aside. Set a griddle pan over a high heat and cook the courgettes for 2 minutes until charred on each side, then tip into the remaining lemon oil mix.

2 Griddle the chops for 3 minutes on each side for pink or until done to your liking, then serve with the courgettes and houmous, if using.

PER SERVING (no houmous) 738 kcals, protein 55g, carbs 3g, fat 56g, sat fat 24g, fibre 1g, sugar 3g, salt 0.42g

Sausage & root veg stovie

These pan-cooked veg go really well with almost anything and have lots more flavour than boiled, so you could also serve them with pork chops or roast chicken pieces.

TAKES 30 MINUTES • SERVES 1

1 stock cube (any type)
1 tbsp sunflower or vegetable oil
1 small onion, halved and thickly sliced
3 thick pork sausages, cut in half
1 large carrot, peeled and cut into chunks
1 large or 2 medium potatoes, skin left on and cut into big chunks
200g/7oz chunk swede, peeled and cut into big chunks (or use another large carrot)

1 Crumble half the stock cube into a mug and top up with boiling water. Stir until dissolved. Heat the oil in a large frying pan, then fry the onion and sausage pieces for 5 minutes until the meat is browned, but not cooked through. Tuck the vegetable chunks around the sausages and onions, and season.

2 Pour over the stock and cover the pan with a lid or large piece of foil, making sure there are no gaps at the edges. Turn the heat to medium and leave for around 25 minutes until the veg are tender and the sausages cooked through. Stir at the end of cooking time – the veg will have caramelised against the bottom of the pan and almost all of the cooking liquid will have been absorbed.

PER SERVING 881 kcals, protein 36g, carbs 73g, fat 52g, sat fat 16g, fibre 11g, sugar 29g, salt 0.63g

Cheesy mushroom omelette

This recipe is so adaptable – use whatever you have left over in your fridge, such as ham, bacon, fresh herbs or sliced cooked potatoes.

TAKES 25 MINUTES ● SERVES 1

1 tbsp olive oil
handful button or chestnut
    mushrooms, sliced
25g/1oz vegetarian Cheddar, grated
small handful parsley leaves, roughly
    chopped
2 eggs, beaten

1 Heat the oil in a small non-stick frying pan. Tip in the mushrooms and fry over a high heat, stirring occasionally for 2–3 minutes, until golden. Lift out of the pan into a bowl and mix with the cheese and parsley.

2 Put the pan back on the heat and swirl the eggs into it. Cook for 1 minute or until set to your liking, swirling with a fork now and again.

3 Spoon the mushroom mix over one half of the omelette. Using a spatula or palette knife, flip the omelette over to cover the mushrooms. Cook for a few moments more, lift on to a plate and serve while it's still hot.

PER SERVING 391 kcals, protein 22g, carbs 0.3g, fat 33g, sat fat 10g, fibre 0.7g, sugar 0.2g, salt 0.90g

Late-night pepperoni & pea rice

Great for an emergency meal, as the ingredients of this spicy sausage recipe are likely to be in your cupboard and everything is measured with just a mug.

TAKES 30 MINUTES ● SERVES 1

1 tbsp olive oil

1 small onion, chopped

handful spicy sausage chunks, such as
     pepperoni or chorizo

½ mug long grain rice

1 vegetable or chicken stock cube

½ mug frozen peas

1 medium egg

1 Heat the oil in a medium pan with a lid, add the onion and fry for 5 minutes until softened. Tip in the sausage chunks and sizzle for a few minutes until they're browned and a bit crispy round the edges. Now add the rice and give everything a good stir. Boil the kettle and pour a mug of boiling water into the pan. Crumble in your stock cube and stir to dissolve completely. Turn the heat down until the liquid is gently bubbling, put a lid on the pan and cook for 15 minutes, stirring occasionally.

2 Stir in the peas, put the lid back on and cook for a further 5 minutes. Beat the egg with a little salt and pepper. Turn the heat up under the rice pan, drop in the egg and stir quickly until the egg has just set. Pile the steaming rice into a bowl and tuck in.

PER SERVING 668 kcals, protein 21g, carbs 94g, fat 26g, sat fat 6g, fibre 2g, salt 3.62g

Salmon rarebit

Canned salmon is not much more expensive than tuna, and has the advantage that it contains healthy omega-3 fats.

TAKES 15 MINUTES • SERVES 1

1 slice granary bread

½ × 212g can Wild Alaskan Pacific salmon, drained and flaked

1–2 spring onions, thinly sliced

2 tbsp cottage cheese

1 tsp grated horseradish (optional)

1 tbsp coarsely grated Red Leicester cheese

watercress and spinach salad, to serve

1 Heat grill to high and toast the bread lightly on both sides.

2 Mix the salmon and spring onions together and season with black pepper only. Spread the mix on to the bread. Mix together the cottage cheese, horseradish (if using) and cheese. Spoon on top of the salmon.

3 Grill on a high shelf for 1 minute, then lower the shelf and continue to grill for a further 3–4 minutes or until the topping starts to brown. Serve straight away with a watercress and spinach salad.

PER SERVING 368 kcals, protein 35g, carbs 19g, fat 15g, sat fat 6g, fibre 2g, sugar 4g, salt 1.1g

Sardines & watercress on toast

Any oily fish works well for this, but sardines are particularly good for you.

TAKES 10 MINUTES • SERVES 1

1 slice granary bread
1 garlic clove, halved
1 vine-ripened tomato, thinly sliced
½ × 115g can Portuguese sardines in spring water, drained
handful organic watercress or wild rocket
balsamic vinegar, for drizzling

1 Lightly toast the bread. Rub the cut side of the garlic over the surface of the toast and arrange the tomato slices on top. Add some seasoning, if you like.
2 Break up the sardines with a fork and arrange on top of the tomato slices. Pile on the watercress and drizzle with balsamic vinegar to serve.

PER SERVING 202 kcals, protein 15g, carbs 23g, fat 6g, sat fat 1g, fibre 3g, sugar none, salt 0.85g

Mexican turkey salad

Making the tortilla bowl is totally optional but it does make your meal for one a bit more fun.

TAKES 25 MINUTES • SERVES 1

1 large flour tortilla
2 tbsp olive oil
juice ½ lime
1 tbsp sliced jalapeños, plus 1 tbsp of vinegar from the jar
handful crisp salad leaves
2 thick slices cooked turkey, shredded
½ avocado, peeled, stoned and cut into chunks
1 tomato, chopped
½ small red onion, sliced
1 tbsp Cheddar cheese, grated
soured cream, to garnish (optional)

1 Heat oven to 220C/200C fan/gas 7. First, make a tortilla basket, if you like. Soften the tortilla in the microwave for a few seconds, then brush with a little of the oil and gently use it to line a small ovenproof bowl. Cover with a foil lining and weigh it down with a slightly smaller ovenproof bowl. Cook for 8–12 minutes until crisp, then allow to cool slightly in the bowl before removing.

2 Make the dressing by mixing the remaining oil, lime juice, vinegar from the jalapeño jar and some salt and pepper. Mix the leaves, turkey, avocado, tomato and red onion, and toss with the dressing. If you're using the tortilla bowl, pile the salad mixture into the tortilla, otherwise just use an ordinary serving bowl. Top with the cheese and jalapeños and a dollop of soured cream, if you like.

PER SERVING 616 kcals, protein 26g, carbs 32g, fat 44g, sat fat 9g, fibre 5g, sugar 9g, salt 1.81g

All-in-one gammon, egg & chips

You can use smoked or unsmoked gammon for this recipe, depending on taste. If you don't fancy the egg, leave it out and swap it for a couple of pineapple rings instead.

TAKES 50 MINUTES • SERVES 1

1 large baking potato, cut into chunky
   chips
1 tbsp olive oil
1 small gammon steak
1 egg

1 Heat oven to 200C/180C fan/gas 6. Spread the chips on a baking sheet and drizzle with the oil and add some salt and pepper. Cook in the oven for 25 minutes, until starting to brown.

2 Remove the baking sheet and turn the chips, pushing them to one side, then put the gammon in the centre and cook for 7 minutes. Take the baking sheet out of the oven and turn the gammon over, then crack the egg into the corner of the tin. Cook for 7 minutes more until the egg is set and the gammon is completely cooked through.

PER SERVING 583 kcals, protein 32g, carbs 34g, fat 36g, sat fat 10g, fibre 3g, sugar 1g, salt 3.91g

Warm chickpea, chilli & feta salad

This colourful vegetarian salad couldn't be easier to make but the end result looks very impressive.

TAKES 15 MINUTES • SERVES 1

1 tbsp olive oil
juice ½ lemon
½ tsp smoked paprika
100g/4oz spinach leaves
1 red pepper, deseeded and sliced
1 red chilli, deseeded and thinly sliced
4 spring onions, sliced
100g/4oz cherry tomatoes, halved
400g can chickpeas, drained and rinsed
40g/1½oz feta or vegetarian
   alternative, crumbled

1 Whisk together 1 teaspoon of the olive oil, the lemon juice, smoked paprika and a little seasoning to make a dressing. Divide the spinach equally between two serving bowls.

2 Heat the remaining olive oil in a non-stick frying pan. Stir-fry the pepper for 5 minutes over a high heat until starting to caramelise at the edges. Add the chilli, spring onions and tomatoes, and stir-fry for 1 minute. Tip in the chickpeas and cook for a further minute, then stir in the dressing.

3 Spoon the hot chickpea mixture over the spinach leaves, then top with the crumbled feta.

PER SERVING 289 kcals, protein 15g, carbs 28g, fat 14g, sat fat 3g, fibre 8g, sugar 8g, salt 1.41g

Sausages with winter veg mash

The mustardy bubble 'n' squeak makes the perfect side dish for ever-popular sausages.

TAKES 20 MINUTES ● SERVES 1

2 sausages (regular or reduced-fat)
1 parsnip
1 large potato
100g/4oz Brussels sprouts
2 tbsp milk
1 tbsp wholegrain mustard

1 Heat grill to high then cook the sausages for 10–12 minutes, turning frequently. Meanwhile, peel and roughly chop the parsnip and potato, then cook in a pan of boiling salted water for about 10 minutes. Shred the sprouts, add to the pan for the last 2–3 minutes and cook until all the vegetables are tender.

2 Drain and mash the vegetables, then beat in the milk and mustard with salt and pepper. Serve with the sausages.

PER SERVING 644 kcals, protein 25g, carbs 67g, fat 33g, sat fat 10g, fibre 14g, sugar 17g, salt 2.48g

Leeky salmon in a parcel

Assemble the parcel a few hours ahead or even in the morning, zap in the microwave, and that's supper ready.

TAKES 20 MINUTES • SERVES 1

1 salmon fillet (about 140g/5oz)
1 small leek
small handful frozen petits pois
2 heaped tbsp crème fraîche, plus
   1 tbsp extra to garnish
1 tbsp chopped fresh tarragon

1 Season the salmon fillet all over. Slice the leek really thinly. Cut a 40cm-square sheet of greaseproof paper and put the salmon fillet in the middle of it. Top with the sliced leek and the peas and crème fraîche. Sprinkle with the tarragon and some salt and pepper to taste.

2 Seal the paper parcel and stand on a microwave-proof plate or baking sheet. Microwave on full power for 5 minutes. Put the contents of the parcel on a plate and top with the extra spoonful of crème fraîche. Serve straight away.

PER SERVING 535 kcals, protein 34g, carbs 8g, fat 41g, sat fat 19g, fibre 3g, salt 0.41g

Roast pork chops with fennel & potatoes

Bulk out a value pack of four pork chops with lots of tasty and healthy vegetables.

TAKES 1 HOUR ● SERVES 4

2 potatoes, cut into 8 wedges
1 fennel bulb, cut into 8 wedges
1 red pepper, halved, deseeded and
    cut into 8
4 fresh thyme sprigs
4 garlic cloves, unpeeled
1 tbsp tomato purée
300ml/½ pint hot chicken stock
4 bone-in pork loin chops

1 Heat oven to 200C/180C fan/gas 6. Put the potatoes, fennel, pepper, thyme and garlic in a large roasting tin. Mix together the tomato purée and stock, then pour into the pan. Tightly cover with foil and cook for 30 minutes. Take out of the oven and increase the temperature to 220C/200C fan/gas 7.
2 Remove the foil and put the pork in the roasting tin, nestling among the veg. Season well and return to the oven for 15–20 minutes more or until the pork is golden brown and cooked through. Serve with the pan juices drizzled over.

PER SERVING 655 kcals, protein 44g, carbs 15g, fat 47g, sat fat 18g, fibre 3g, sugar 3g, salt 0.54g

Chicken, potato & green bean curry

Using chicken thighs over breast will save half the money and thighs are actually better suited to a dish like this.

TAKES 40 MINUTES • SERVES 4

1 tbsp sunflower oil
1 onion, chopped
6 skinless chicken thigh fillets, cubed
2 potatoes, cut into small cubes
2 tbsp mild curry paste
500g/1lb 2oz tomato passata
200g/7oz fine green beans
150g pot natural yogurt
plain rice or naan bread, to serve

1 Heat the oil in a large frying pan and cook the onion and chicken together over a medium heat for 5 minutes until the onion is soft. Add the potatoes, curry paste and passata, bring to the boil, then cover and gently simmer for 15 minutes.

2 Add the beans and a splash of water and cook for 10–15 minutes more until all the vegetables are tender and the chicken is cooked through. Remove from the heat and stir in the yogurt. Serve with rice or naan.

PER SERVING 333 kcals, protein 36g, carbs 26g, fat 10g, sat fat 3g, fibre 3g, sugar 10g, salt 1.34g

One-pot chicken & bacon stew

However many you are cooking for, make a big batch of this delicious stew and freeze any leftovers.

TAKES 2 HOURS • SERVES 8

3 tbsp olive oil
16 chicken pieces on the bone (about 3kg/6lb 8oz total)
140g/5oz smoked bacon, chopped
4 medium carrots, thickly sliced
2 onions, roughly chopped
2 tbsp plain flour
1 tbsp tomato purée
75ml/2½fl oz white wine vinegar or cider vinegar
1 litre/1¾ pints chicken stock
2 bay leaves
4 tbsp double cream or crème fraîche
600g/1lb 5oz small new potatoes, halved
12 large white mushrooms, quartered
chopped herbs, such as parsley, tarragon or chives, to sprinkle

1 Heat oven to 200C/180C fan/gas 6. Heat the oil in a large flameproof casserole with a lid. Fry the chicken pieces in batches until well browned, then transfer to a plate. Sizzle the bacon in the casserole for a few minutes until beginning to crisp. Stir in the carrots and onions, then cook for 5 minutes until starting to soften. Stir in the flour and tomato purée, and cook for 1 minute more. Finally, splash in the vinegar and stir well.

2 Pour in the stock and bring to a simmer. Add the bay, cream and seasoning. Slide in the chicken pieces and scatter over the potatoes, turning everything over a few times so that the potatoes are immersed in the sauce. Pop the lid on and put in the oven. After 40 minutes, remove from the oven and stir in the mushrooms. Cover again and cook in the oven for 10 minutes more until the chicken is cooked through and tender but not completely falling off the bone. Sprinkle over the herbs and serve.

PER SERVING 736 kcals, protein 60g, carbs 21g, fat 46g, sat fat 14g, fibre 4g, sugar 7g, salt 1.74g

Greek lamb with potatoes & olives

If fresh oregano is a little tricky to find just swap it for 1 tablespoon dried.

TAKES 1½ HOURS • SERVES 4

800g/1lb 12oz medium-sized potatoes, skin on, thinly sliced
4 large tomatoes, thinly sliced
1 aubergine, thinly sliced
4 garlic cloves, chopped
3 tbsp oregano leaves, plus extra for sprinkling
85g/3oz pitted black olives, halved
5 tbsp olive oil, plus a drizzle
100g/4oz feta, crumbled
4 lamb steaks
crusty bread, to serve

1 Heat oven to 200C/180C fan/gas 6. Layer up half the potatoes, tomatoes and aubergine in a baking dish, scattering with garlic, oregano and olives, and drizzling with oil and seasoning as you go.

2 Scatter over the feta, then repeat the layers until all the ingredients are used up. Finish with a layer of potatoes and a little oil.

3 Bake for 50 minutes or until the veg are tender (cover with foil if they're getting too brown). Top with the lamb steaks, rubbing with a little more oil and seasoning. Bake for 15–20 minutes more until the lamb is cooked. Allow to rest and cool a bit before sprinkling with oregano and serving with crusty bread.

PER SERVING 772 kcals, protein 38g, carbs 42g, fat 51g, sat fat 19g, fibre 6g, sugar 8g, salt 2.03g

Easy paella

Making this cheats' version of a hard-to-get-right Spanish classic couldn't be easier as it's all cooked in one pan.

TAKES 40 MINUTES ● SERVES 4

1 tbsp olive oil
1 onion, chopped
1 tsp each hot smoked paprika and dried thyme
300g/10oz paella or risotto rice
3 tbsp dry sherry or white wine (optional)
400g can chopped tomatoes with garlic
900ml/1½ pints chicken stock
400g bag frozen mixed seafood, defrosted
juice ½ lemon, other half cut into wedges to garnish
handful flat-leaf parsley, roughly chopped, to scatter

1 Heat the oil in a large frying pan with a lid, add the onion and soften for 5 minutes. Stir in the paprika, thyme and rice, stir for 1 minute, then splash in the sherry or wine, if using. Once it has evaporated, stir in the tomatoes and stock. Season and cook, uncovered, for about 15 minutes, stirring now and again until the rice is almost tender and still surrounded with some liquid.

2 Stir the seafood into the pan and cover with the lid. Simmer for 5 minutes, or until the prawns are cooked through and the rice is tender. Squeeze over the lemon juice, scatter with parsley and serve with extra lemon wedges on the side.

PER SERVING 431 kcals, protein 34g, carbs 66g, fat 5g, sat fat 1g, fibre 3g, sugar 5g, salt 2.14g

Red Thai meatball curry

A new, packed-with-flavour idea that will transform a packet of minced beef.

TAKES 40 MINUTES • SERVES 4

500g pack lean minced beef (10% fat)
2 red chillies, 1 chopped, 1 sliced
thumb-size piece ginger, grated
1 egg
1 tbsp sunflower or vegetable oil
1–1½ tbsp Thai red curry paste
    (depending on how spicy you like it)
400ml can reduced-fat coconut milk
225g can bamboo shoots, drained
    and rinsed
140g/5oz fine green beans, trimmed
juice 1 lime, plus extra wedges to
    garnish
20g pack basil
basmati rice or rice noodles, to serve

1 Put the mince into a large bowl with the chopped chilli, ginger and egg, then season generously. Mix well with your hands, then shape into 20 meatballs. These can be made and chilled up to a day ahead.

2 Heat the oil in a large non-stick frying pan, then brown the meatballs for 5 minutes. Tip on to a plate. Add the curry paste, fry for 1 minute, then pour in the coconut milk and half a can of water. Bring back to the boil and stir to make a smooth sauce.

3 Return the meatballs to the pan with the bamboo shoots and beans. Simmer for 5 minutes until the beans are just tender and the meatballs are cooked through. To serve, season the sauce with some salt and pepper and the lime juice, then tear in the basil leaves. Scatter with the sliced chilli and serve with rice or noodles and the lime wedges for squeezing over.

PER SERVING 371 kcals, protein 31g, carbs 4g, fat 26g, sat fat 13g, fibre 2g, sugar 2g, salt 0.79g

Quick steak & mushroom stroganoff

This treat-for-two also works with sliced pork, but if you use this meat choose a lean cut like loin or fillet.

TAKES 30 MINUTES ● SERVES 2

1 tbsp oil
1 red onion, chopped
2 garlic cloves, chopped
1 tsp paprika
1 green pepper, chopped
200g/7oz mushrooms, sliced
2 tbsp red wine vinegar
150ml/¼ pint beef stock
200g/7oz lean rump steak, sliced and
    all fat removed
150ml/¼ pint fat-free fromage frais
rice or tagliatelle, to serve

1 Heat the oil in a pan and fry the onion for a few minutes, until soft. Add the garlic and paprika, and cook for 1–2 minutes until fragrant. Add the pepper and mushrooms, and fry for 5–8 minutes, until softened.

2 Add the vinegar, boil to reduce until almost evaporated, then pour over the stock and bubble for a few minutes until thickened slightly. Add the beef and cook for 2–3 minutes depending on how rare you like it, then stir in the fromage frais and season. Serve with rice or some tagliatelle.

PER SERVING 271 kcals, protein 33g, carbs 11g, fat 11g, sat fat 3g, fibre 3g, sugar 8g, salt 0.45g

One-pan roast dinner

This all-in-one roast contributes to vitamin A and C intake, which is especially important for those who don't eat much fresh fruit and veg.

TAKES 1 HOUR 40 MINUTES

● **SERVES 4**

1.5kg/3lb 5oz whole chicken

1 lemon, halved

50g/2oz softened butter

2 tsp dried mixed herbs

750g/1lb 10oz potatoes, chopped into roastie size

about 7 carrots, roughly 500g/1lb 2oz, each chopped into 2–3 chunks

2 tbsp olive oil

100g/4oz frozen peas

300ml/½ pint chicken stock

1 tsp Marmite

1 Heat oven to 220C/200C fan/gas 7. Snip the string or elastic off the chicken if it's tied up, then put in a big roasting tin. Shove the lemon halves into the cavity. Rub the butter, herbs and some seasoning all over the chicken. Put the potatoes and carrots around it, drizzle everything with oil, season and toss together.

2 Roast for 20 minutes, then turn the oven down to 200C/180C fan/gas 6 and roast for 50 minutes more. Stir the peas, stock and Marmite into the veg in the tin, then return to the oven for a further 10 minutes.

PER SERVING 845 kcals, protein 55g, carbs 45g, fat 51g, sat fat 17g, fibre 7g, sugar 11g, salt 1.1g

Hot & sour pork & pepper stir-fry

Treat this recipe as a blueprint and add your favourite veg to it. Green beans, broccoli and asparagus when in season would all work well.

TAKES 35 MINUTES • SERVES 2

1 tbsp sesame seeds
1 tsp sunflower oil
250g/9oz pork fillet, cut into finger-width strips
1 red and 1 yellow pepper, deseeded and sliced
2 tsp cornflour
2 tsp soy sauce
juice 1 lime
2 tbsp clear honey
½ red chilli, deseeded and sliced
steamed rice, to serve

1 Dry-fry the sesame seeds until toasted and golden, then tip into a small bowl and set aside. Heat the oil in a non-stick frying pan or wok, add the pork and peppers, and stir-fry for 5–6 minutes over a high heat until the pork is lightly browned and cooked right through.

2 Mix the cornflour and soy sauce together in a bowl, then add the lime juice, honey, chilli and sesame seeds, plus 6 tablespoons cold water. Pour into the pan or wok and cook until the sauce has slightly thickened, tossing the pan or wok to coat the pork and peppers. Serve with steamed rice.

PER SERVING 338 kcals, protein 30g, carbs 24g, fat 14g, sat fat 4g, fibre 3g, sugar 20g, salt 1.1g

Spanish bean stew

There are two types of the spicy Spanish sausage chorizo; for this easy stew you need the thumb-sized cooking type.

TAKES 40 MINUTES • **SERVES 4**

1 tbsp olive oil

200g/7oz chorizo sausage, thickly
   sliced

1 onion, chopped

400g/14oz skinless chicken thigh fillets,
   cubed

1 tomato, roughly chopped

410g can cannellini beans, drained
   and rinsed

1 large potato, cut into small cubes

500ml/18fl oz hot chicken stock

4 tbsp chopped flat-leaf parsley leaves

1 Heat the oil in a large pan. Cook the chorizo, onion and chicken over a high heat for 5 minutes. Add the tomato and cook for a further 2–3 minutes until pulpy.

2 Stir in the beans, potato and stock. Bring to the boil, then cover and gently simmer for 20 minutes until the potato is soft and the chicken cooked through. Stir through the parsley and serve.

PER SERVING 433 kcals, protein 43g, carbs 25g, fat 19g, sat fat 6g, fibre 5g, sugar 5g, salt 3.05g

Sticky pork with cranberries

If you have some cranberry sauce lurking in your cupboard, use it to make this easy pork dish.

TAKES 40 MINUTES ● SERVES 4

1 tbsp plain flour
500g/1lb 2oz pork tenderloin, sliced
 into steaks
1 tbsp olive oil
2 red onions, cut into wedges
400ml/14fl oz chicken stock
4 tbsp cranberry sauce
1 tbsp honey
mash or jacket potatoes and
 vegetables, to serve

1 Season the flour and dust the pork steaks. Heat the oil in a large frying pan, then cook the pork for 3–4 minutes each side until browned and cooked through. Transfer to a plate and set aside.
2 Add the red onion wedges to the pan and fry for 5–8 minutes until soft and starting to turn golden. Stir in the stock, cranberry sauce and honey, and simmer for 10 minutes. Return the pork with any resting juices and gently cook for 1–2 minutes until hot through. Serve with some mash or jacket potatoes and vegetables.

PER SERVING 281 kcals, protein 31g, carbs 14g, fat 11g, sat fat 3g, fibre 1g, sugar 11g, salt 0.43g

Honey, mustard & crème fraîche baked chicken

Fresh tarragon is the classic herb to use in a chicken dish like this, but there is already enough flavour here to make it totally optional.

TAKES 50 MINUTES • SERVES 4

4 tbsp crème fraîche
2 tbsp grainy mustard
2 garlic cloves, crushed
150ml/¼ pint chicken stock
8 skin-on chicken drumsticks and
  thighs
500g/1lb 2oz baby potatoes
200g/7oz green beans
2 tbsp clear honey
½ small bunch tarragon, roughly
  chopped, to garnish (optional)

1 Heat oven to 200C/180C fan/gas 6. Mix together the crème fraîche, mustard, garlic and stock with some seasoning. Arrange the chicken, skin-side up, in a roasting tin just large enough for the chicken and vegetables.

2 Tuck the potatoes and beans in among the chicken pieces. Pour over the stock mixture then season the chicken and drizzle with honey. Bake for 40–45 minutes until the chicken is cooked through and the potatoes tender. Scatter over the tarragon, if using, before serving.

PER SERVING 695 kcals, protein 53g, carbs 29g, fat 42g, sat fat 14g, fibre 3g, sugar 9g, salt 0.97g

Thai coconut & veg broth

Get a taste of Thailand with this quick and easy noodle soup cooked in one pan.
If you're cooking this for meat-eaters, try adding shredded leftover roast chicken.

TAKES 25 MINUTES • SERVES 4

1½ tbsp Thai red curry paste
1 tsp vegetable oil
1 litre/1¾ pints vegetable stock
400ml can half-fat coconut milk
2 tsp brown sugar
175g/6oz medium egg noodles
2 carrots, cut into matchsticks
½ head Chinese leaf cabbage, sliced
½ × 300g bag beansprouts
6 cherry tomatoes, halved
juice 1 lime
3 spring onions, halved, then finely
   sliced lengthways, to sprinkle
handful coriander, roughly chopped,
   to garnish

1 Put the curry paste in a large pan or wok with the oil. Fry for 1 minute until fragrant. Tip in the vegetable stock, coconut milk and brown sugar. Simmer for 3 minutes.
2 Add the noodles, carrots and Chinese leaf, and simmer for 4–6 minutes, until all are tender. Mix in the beansprouts and tomatoes. Add lime juice to taste and some extra seasoning, if you like. Spoon into bowls and sprinkle with the spring onions and coriander.

PER SERVING 338 kcals, protein 10g, carbs 46g, fat 14g, sat fat 7g, fibre 5g, sugar 12g, salt 1.19g

Oven-baked leek & bacon risotto

A one-pot risotto you don't need to stand over for half an hour? Got to be a midweek winner.

TAKES 40 MINUTES ● **SERVES 4**

1 tbsp olive oil

6 rashers smoked back bacon, roughly chopped

2 leeks, halved lengthways and finely sliced

250g/9oz risotto rice

700ml/1¼ pints hot chicken or vegetable stock

175g/6oz frozen peas

3 tbsp soft cheese

zest 1 lemon

1 Heat oven to 200C/180C fan/ gas 6. Tip the oil into an ovenproof casserole dish, add the bacon and fry for 2 minutes. Add the leeks and cook until soft, but not coloured, for about 4–5 minutes. Tip in the rice and cook for 1 minute more. Pour over the stock. Cover and put in the oven for 20 minutes, stirring halfway through.

2 When the rice is just tender and all the liquid is absorbed, remove from the oven and stir in the peas. Put back in the oven for 2 minutes more. Remove and stir in the cheese. Add the zest, season, stir and serve immediately.

PER SERVING 424 kcals, protein 22g, carbs 55g, fat 14g, sat fat 5g, fibre 5g, sugar 3g, salt 2.34g

Bean & pasta stew with meatballs

A comforting, filling and quick stew that's also light on the pocket.

TAKES 55 MINUTES ● SERVES 4

6–8 pack pork sausages
1 tbsp olive oil
2 onions, finely chopped
3 celery sticks, diced
2 carrots, diced
3 garlic cloves, finely chopped
400g can chopped tomatoes
1 litre/1¾ pints chicken stock
175g/6oz macaroni
410g can cannellini beans, drained
   and rinsed
handful flat-leaf parsley, chopped

1 Snip the ends off the sausages and squeeze out the meat. Roll into rough walnut-sized meatballs. Heat half the oil in a large, wide pan and fry until browned, around 10 minutes. Remove from the pan and set aside. Add the rest of the oil to the pan. Tip in the onions, celery and carrots, and fry for 10 minutes until soft. Add the garlic and cook for 1 minute more. Tip in the tomatoes and stock. Bring to the boil and simmer for 10 minutes.

2 Stir in the macaroni and add the meatballs. Simmer for about 10 minutes until the pasta is cooked and the meatballs are cooked through. Stir in the beans and heat until piping hot. Season, mix in the parsley, and serve.

PER SERVING 688 kcals, protein 34g, carbs 67g, fat 33g, sat fat 10g, fibre 10g, sugar 15g, salt 3.6g

One-pot mushroom & potato curry

When making a vegetarian curry with a paste, read the label carefully to make sure it doesn't contain anything non-veggie.

TAKES 30 MINUTES • SERVES 4

1 tbsp olive oil

1 onion, roughly chopped

1 large potato, chopped into small chunks

1 aubergine, trimmed and chopped into chunks

250g/9oz button mushrooms

2–4 tbsp curry paste (depending on how hot you like it)

150ml/¼ pint vegetable stock

400ml can reduced-fat coconut milk

chopped coriander leaves, to garnish

rice or naan bread, to serve

1 Heat the oil in a large pan and add the onion and potato. Cover, then cook over a low heat for 5 minutes until the potato starts to soften. Throw in the aubergine and mushrooms, and cook for a few more minutes.

2 Stir in the curry paste, pour over the stock and coconut milk. Bring to the boil, then simmer for 10 minutes or until the potato is tender. Sprinkle over the coriander and serve with rice or naan bread on the side.

PER SERVING 212 kcals, protein 5g, carbs 15g, fat 15g, sat fat 9g, fibre 3g, sugar 5g, salt 0.71g

Sweetcorn & smoked haddock chowder

This main-meal soup makes the most of cheaper-than-fresh frozen fish fillets.

TAKES 20 MINUTES • SERVES 2

knob of butter

2 rashers streaky bacon, chopped

1 onion, finely chopped

500ml/18fl oz milk

350g/12oz potatoes (about 2 medium), cut into small cubes

300g/10oz frozen smoked haddock fillets

140g/5oz frozen sweetcorn

chopped flat-leaf parsley, to garnish (optional)

crusty bread, to serve

1 Heat the butter in a large pan. Tip in the bacon, then cook until starting to brown. Add the onion, cook until soft, then pour over the milk and stir through the potatoes. Bring to the boil, then simmer for 5 minutes.

2 Add the haddock, then leave to cook gently for another 10 minutes. By now the fish should have defrosted so you can break it into large chunks. Stir through the sweetcorn, then cook for another few minutes until the fish is cooked through and the sweetcorn has defrosted. Scatter over parsley, if using. Serve with plenty of crusty bread.

PER SERVING 550 kcals, protein 47g, carbs 59g, fat 16g, sat fat 7g, fibre 4g, sugar 18g, salt 3.92g

Spicy root & lentil casserole

The potatoes in this recipe take on the spicy flavours beautifully, making it a tasty and filling veggie supper.

TAKES 45 MINUTES • SERVES 4

2 tbsp sunflower or vegetable oil
1 onion, chopped
2 garlic cloves, crushed
700g/1lb 9oz potatoes, peeled and cut into chunks
4 carrots, thickly sliced
2 parsnips, thickly sliced
2 tbsp curry paste or powder
1 litre/1¾ pints vegetable stock
100g/4oz dried red split lentils
small bunch fresh coriander, roughly chopped
low-fat yogurt and naan bread, to serve

1 Heat the oil in a large pan, then cook the onion and garlic over a medium heat for 3–4 minutes until softened, stirring occasionally. Tip in the potatoes, carrots and parsnips, turn up the heat, then cook for 6–7 minutes, stirring, until the vegetables are golden.

2 Stir in the curry paste or powder, pour in the stock, then bring to the boil. Reduce the heat, add the lentils, then cover and simmer for 15–20 minutes until the lentils and vegetables are tender and the sauce has thickened.

3 Stir in most of the coriander, season, then heat for a minute or so. Serve with yogurt, the rest of the coriander sprinkled over and some naan bread.

PER SERVING 378 kcals, protein 14g, carbs 64g, fat 9g, sat fat 1g, fibre 10g, sugar none, salt 1.24g

Five-a-day tagine

Shop for the vegetables in this recipe at the local markets and you can pick up some great bargains.

TAKES 45 MINUTES • SERVES 4

4 carrots, cut into chunks
4 small parsnips or 3 large, cut into chunks
3 red onions, cut into wedges
2 red peppers, deseeded and cut into chunks
2 tbsp olive oil
1 tsp each ground cumin, paprika, cinnamon and mild chilli powder
400g can chopped tomatoes
2 small handfuls soft dried apricots
2 tsp honey
couscous or jacket potatoes, to serve

1 Heat oven to 200C/180C fan/gas 6. Scatter the veg over a couple of baking sheets, drizzle with half the oil, season, then rub the oil over the veg with your hands to coat. Roast for 30 minutes until tender and beginning to brown.

2 Meanwhile, fry the spices in the remaining oil for 1 minute – they should sizzle and start to smell aromatic. Tip in the tomatoes, apricots, honey and a can of water. Simmer for 5 minutes until the sauce is slightly reduced and the apricots plump, then stir in the veg and some seasoning. Serve with couscous or jacket potatoes.

PER SERVING 272 kcals, protein 7g, carbs 45g, fat 8g, sat fat 1g, fibre 12g, sugar 32g, salt 0.35g

Peppered-mackerel fish cakes

These clever fish cakes make a whole new meal out of leftover mashed potato.

TAKES 35 MINUTES ● **SERVES 4**

300g/10oz cold mashed potato
6 spring onions, thinly sliced
1 tbsp horseradish sauce, optional
250g/9oz peppered mackerel fillets,
    skinned and flaked
2 tbsp plain flour
1 egg, beaten
85g/3oz dried breadcrumbs
sunflower oil, for frying (optional)
salad and lemon wedges, to serve
    and garnish

1 In a large bowl, mix together the potato, spring onions, horseradish and mackerel, then shape into eight even-sized cakes. Roll the fish cakes in the flour, shaking off any excess, then dip in the egg, followed by the breadcrumbs. Cover and chill until ready to cook. Can be prepared up to a day ahead, or frozen.

2 Gently grill or shallow-fry the fish cakes for 5–6 minutes on each side until crunchy, golden brown and hot all the way through. Serve with salad and lemon wedges.

PER SERVING (grilled) 427 kcals, protein 18g, carbs 32g, fat 26g, sat fat 5g, fibre 2g, sugar 2g, salt 1.76g

Moroccan chicken with sweet potato mash

This recipe also works with lamb chops or salmon fillets – just change the cooking time accordingly.

TAKES 35 MINUTES ● SERVES 4

1kg/2lb 4oz sweet potatoes, cubed
1 tsp ground cinnamon
1 tsp ground cumin
4 boneless skinless chicken breasts
2 tbsp olive oil
1 onion, thinly sliced
1 fat garlic clove, crushed
200ml/7fl oz chicken stock
2 tsp clear honey
juice ½ lemon
handful green olives, pitted or whole
20g pack coriander, leaves chopped

1 Boil the potatoes in salted water for 15 minutes or until tender. Mix the spices with the seasoning, then sprinkle all over the chicken. Heat 1 tablespoon of the oil in a large frying pan, then brown the chicken for 3 minutes on each side until golden.

2 Lift the chicken out of the pan. Add the onion and garlic, and cook for 5 minutes until softened. Add the stock, honey, lemon juice and olives, return the chicken to the pan, then simmer for 10 minutes until the sauce is syrupy and the chicken cooked.

3 Mash the potatoes with the remaining tablespoon of oil and season. Thickly slice each chicken breast and stir the coriander through the sauce. Serve the chicken and sauce over the mash.

PER SERVING 460 kcals, protein 39g, carbs 59g, fat 9g, sat fat 2g, fibre 7g, sugar 18g, salt 1.11g

Crowd-pleaser cottage pie

Make two pies and invite everyone round for some food before a big night out, or just freeze one for another day.

TAKES 2 HOURS ● SERVES 10

3 tbsp olive oil
1.25kg/2lb 12oz minced beef
2 onions, finely chopped
3 carrots, chopped
2 garlic cloves, finely chopped
3 tbsp plain flour
1 tbsp tomato purée
850ml/1½ pints beef stock
4 tbsp Worcestershire sauce
2 bay leaves

FOR THE MASH

1.8kg/4lb potatoes, chopped
225ml/8fl oz milk
25g/1oz butter
200g/7oz strong Cheddar, grated
a little freshly grated nutmeg

1 Heat 1 tablespoon of the oil in a pan and fry the mince until browned – you may need to do this in batches – then set aside. Put the rest of the oil into the pan, add the vegetables and cook gently until soft, about 20 minutes. Add the garlic, flour and tomato purée, increase the heat and cook for a few minutes, then return the beef to the pan. Add the stock, Worcestershire sauce and bay leaves. Bring to a simmer and cook, uncovered, for 45 minutes. By this time the gravy should be thick. Season well, then discard the bay leaves.

2 Meanwhile, in a large pan, cover the potatoes in cold water, bring to the boil and simmer until tender. Drain and mash with the milk, butter and three-quarters of the cheese, then season with the nutmeg and some salt and pepper. Heat oven to 220C/200C fan/gas 7.

3 Spoon the meat into two ovenproof dishes. Spoon on the mash and sprinkle with the remaining cheese. Cook for 25–30 minutes.

PER SERVING 600 kcals, protein 37g, carbs 40g, fat 34g, sat fat 16g, fibre 4g, sugar 7g, salt 1.15g

Vegetable curry for a crowd

This curry is great for feeding a group of mates, although the recipe can easily be halved. It also keeps well in the fridge for a few days or can be frozen.

TAKES 1 HOUR • SERVES 8

1 large potato, diced
1 small butternut squash, peeled, deseeded and diced
1 aubergine, diced
6 tbsp tikka masala curry paste
3 tbsp vegetable oil
2 onions, sliced
680g–700g jar tomato passata
400g can coconut milk
2 red peppers, sliced
2 courgettes, diced
few coriander sprigs, to garnish
rice or naan bread, to serve

1 Heat oven to 200C/180C fan/gas 6. Toss the potato, squash and aubergine with 2 tablespoons of the curry paste and 2 tablespoons of the oil in a large roasting tin. Season, then roast for 30 minutes.

2 Meanwhile, make the sauce. Fry the onions in the remaining oil in a large pan until softened and golden – add a splash of water if they start to dry out. Stir in the remaining curry paste, cook for 3 minutes, then add the passata, coconut milk and 100ml/3½fl oz water. Simmer for a few minutes.

3 When the vegetables are roasted, tip them into the sauce with the peppers and courgettes. Simmer for 10–15 minutes until tender. Scatter with coriander and serve with rice or some naan bread.

PER SERVING 263 kcals, protein 5g, carbs 25g, fat 17g, sat fat 8g, fibre 4g, sugar 14g, salt 1.28g

Big-batch Bolognese

Take advantage of special offers on packs of mince and make enough sauce to feed all your friends and still have some left to freeze.

TAKES 2 HOURS • SERVES 12

4 tbsp olive oil
6 smoked rashers bacon, chopped
4 onions, finely chopped
3 carrots, finely chopped
4 celery sticks, finely chopped
8 garlic cloves, crushed
2 tbsp dried mixed herbs
2 bay leaves
500g/1lb 2oz mushrooms, sliced
1.5kg/3lb 5oz lean minced beef
6 × 400g cans chopped tomatoes
6 tbsp tomato purée
large glass red wine (optional)
4 tbsp red wine vinegar
1 tbsp caster sugar
grated Parmesan, to garnish
pasta, to serve

1 Heat the oil in a very large pan. Gently cook the bacon, onions, carrots and celery for 20 minutes until golden. Add the garlic, herbs, bay and mushrooms, then cook for 2 minutes more.

2 Heat a large frying pan until really hot. Crumble in just enough mince to cover the pan, cook until brown, then tip in with the veg. Continue to fry the mince in batches until used up. Tip the tomatoes and purée in with the mince and veg. Rinse the cans out with the red wine, if you have some, or with a little water, then add to the pan with the vinegar and sugar. Season generously and bring to a simmer. Simmer slowly for 1 hour until thick and saucy and the mince is tender. Serve with pasta and a little Parmesan.

PER SERVING 295 kcals, protein 34g, carbs 13g, fat 12g, sat fat 4g, fibre 4g, sugar 11g, salt 0.87g

Roast pork belly & crackling

Pork belly has the double bonus of being not only one of the cheapest cuts of pork but also the best for making great crackling.

TAKES 3 HOURS, PLUS MARINATING

- **SERVES 6**

2 tbsp fennel seeds
1 tsp black peppercorns
pinch flaked sea salt
1 small bunch thyme, leaves only
3 garlic cloves
3 tbsp olive oil
1.5–2kg/3lb 5oz–4lb 8oz piece boneless
  pork belly, skin scored
2 lemons
braised cabbage and roast potatoes,
  to serve

1 Toast the fennel seeds and peppercorns in a dry frying pan for a couple of minutes. Pound them together in a pestle and mortar with some flaked sea salt, the thyme and garlic to make a paste. Mix with 2 tablespoons of the oil and rub all over the flesh of the pork. Cover and chill, leaving to marinate for a few hours or overnight.

2 When ready to cook, rub the skin of the joint with plenty of salt and the remaining oil. Sit on a wire rack in a roasting tin and roast at 200C/180C fan/gas 6 for 30 minutes. After this time, squeeze the lemons over the skin and turn the heat down to 180C/160C fan/gas 4. Roast for a further 2 hours. Finally, turn the heat back up to 220C/200C fan/gas 7 and give it a final blast for another 30 minutes or so, to finish the crackling. Allow to rest somewhere warm for 20 minutes. Carve up into chunks or slices and serve with braised cabbage and roast potatoes.

PER SERVING 585 kcals, protein 45g, carbs 2g, fat 44g, sat fat 16g, fibre none, sugar none, salt 0.83g

Italian sausage stew with rosemary–garlic mash

Make more out of the classic sausage-and-mash combo with a few Italian touches.

TAKES 1 HOUR • SERVES 4

8 good-quality pork sausages
2 tbsp olive oil
2 carrots, finely chopped
2 celery sticks, finely chopped
1 onion, finely chopped
2 rosemary sprigs, 1 chopped
3 garlic cloves, roughly chopped
175g/6oz dried green lentils, rinsed
400g can chopped tomatoes
700ml/1¼ pint stock
1kg/2lb 4oz potatoes, cut into chunks
150ml/¼ pint milk

1 Fry the sausages in 1 tablespoon of the oil in a casserole dish until brown. Remove. Tip in the carrots, celery and onion, and cook for 10 minutes, adding the chopped rosemary and half the garlic for the final minute. Add the lentils, tomatoes and stock. Return the sausages, bring to the boil, cover, and simmer for 20 minutes. Remove the lid and cook for a further 10–15 minutes until the lentils are soft. Season.

2 Meanwhile, boil the potatoes until tender. In another pan, heat the milk with the remaining garlic and rosemary until just about to boil, then turn off the heat. Drain the potatoes well.

3 Sieve the hot milk over the rest of the potatoes and mash with the remaining oil, then season. Serve with the stew.

PER SERVING 616 kcals, protein 27g, carbs 67g, fat 29g, sat fat 8g, fibre 9g, sugar 12g, salt 3.91g

Mixed-bean chilli with wedges

Cheap, easy, filling and full of flavour, chilli has to be one of the best student dishes there is.

TAKES 50 MINUTES ● **SERVES 4**

4 medium baking potatoes, unpeeled, each cut into 8 wedges
4 tsp olive oil
1 red onion, roughly chopped
1 yellow pepper, roughly chopped
1 tbsp Cajun spice mix
2 × 410g cans mixed pulses in water, drained and rinsed
400g can chopped tomatoes
150ml/¼ pint vegetable stock
4 tbsp reduced-fat soured cream

1 Heat oven to 220C/200C fan/gas 7. Toss the potato wedges in 2 teaspoons of the oil and spread out in a single layer on a large baking sheet. Cook for 30–35 minutes, turning halfway, until tender and golden brown.

2 Meanwhile, for the chilli, put the remaining oil into a casserole dish and fry the onion and pepper for 5 minutes. Add the Cajun spice, pulses, tomatoes and stock. Cover and simmer for 15–20 minutes. Ladle the chilli into four bowls, top each with 1 tablespoon of the soured cream and serve with the wedges.

PER SERVING 353 kcals, protein 16g, carbs 57g, fat 8g, sat fat 2g, fibre 12g, sugar 12g, salt 0.35g

Mexican veggie wraps

Place all the elements in the middle of the table and let everyone make their own wrap with this cutlery-free supper.

TAKES 40 MINUTES • SERVES 4

½ butternut squash, peeled, cut into large wedges
1 red chilli, deseeded and chopped
1 tbsp Cajun spice mix
1 tbsp oil
400g can refried beans
2 tomatoes, chopped
4 tbsp natural yogurt
zest and juice 1 lime
8 flour tortilla wraps
50g bag rocket

1 Heat oven to 200C/180C fan/gas 6. In a roasting tin, toss the squash with the chilli, spices, oil and some seasoning, then roast for 25 minutes until tender. Gently heat the refried beans with the chopped tomatoes until warmed through. Mix the yogurt with the lime zest and juice.

2 Warm the wraps according to the pack instructions and spread with a thin layer of beans. Top with the squash mix, some rocket and a dollop of lime yogurt.

PER SERVING 427 kcals, protein 15g, carbs 81g, fat 6g, sat fat 1g, fibre 4g, sugar 8g, salt 1.86g

Homemade fish-finger sarnies

Making your own fish fingers not only tastes better but makes these burgers superhealthy.

TAKES 45 MINUTES ● **SERVES 4**

300g/10oz skinless white fish fillet
1 egg, beaten
50g/2oz cornflakes, bashed into
    crumbs
3 sweet potatoes, cut into chunky
    chips
1 tbsp olive oil
small handful mixed salad leaves
4 small wholemeal buns
1 lemon, cut into wedges, to garnish

FOR THE TARTARE SAUCE

2 tbsp light mayonnaise
1 tbsp chopped gherkins
1 tsp capers, rinsed and chopped

1 Heat oven to 200C/180C fan/gas 6. Cut the fish into four equal-sized portions. Dip in the beaten egg, coat in the cornflakes, then chill for 10 minutes. Toss the sweet potatoes in the oil and some seasoning, then cook for 20 minutes on a baking sheet.

2 Meanwhile, make the tartare sauce. Mix all the ingredients with some seasoning, then set aside.

3 Remove the sweet potato chips, turn them over, add the fish to the baking sheet and cook everything for around 15 minutes more, turning the fish halfway through. When cooked, add a few salad leaves to each bun, top with a fish finger and a dollop of tartare, and serve with the chips and lemon wedges for squeezing over.

PER SERVING 410 kcals, protein 23g, carbs 63g, fat 9g, sat fat 2g, fibre 6g, sugar 12g, salt 1.47g

Lamb meatballs with rosemary tomato sauce

Ready-made meatballs save you time and effort and are nothing more than meat and seasoning that has been ready-rolled for you.

TAKES 45 MINUTES ● SERVES 4

2 tsp olive oil
1 pack 12 ready-made lamb meatballs
  (about 450g/1lb)
4 onions, finely sliced
4 garlic cloves, finely sliced
1 tbsp finely chopped rosemary leaves,
  plus extra to sprinkle
2 × 400g cans chopped tomatoes
400g/14oz pasta, cooked, to serve

1 Heat 1 teaspoon of the oil in a large frying pan. Add the meatballs and cook, turning often, until browned. Remove from the pan.

2 Tip the onions into the pan with the remaining oil and a pinch of salt, and cook until very soft, 10–15 minutes. Add the garlic and rosemary, and cook for 2 minutes more.

3 Add the tomatoes and return the meatballs to the pan. Simmer for 10 minutes until the sauce has thickened and the meatballs are cooked through. Season and serve with the pasta, sprinkled with the extra rosemary.

PER SERVING 311 kcals, protein 23g, carbs 22g, fat 15g, sat fat 6g, fibre 5g, sugar 11g, salt 1.84g

Chicken & bean enchiladas

Great gathering food, these will be popular with everyone so it's worth making a lot.

TAKES 1 HOUR • MAKES 10

3 tbsp olive oil

2 red onions, sliced

2 red peppers, sliced

3 red chillies, 2 deseeded and chopped, 1 sliced

small bunch coriander, stalks finely chopped, leaves roughly chopped – plus extra to garnish (optional)

2 garlic cloves, crushed

1 tbsp ground coriander

1 tbsp cumin seeds

6 boneless skinless chicken breasts, cut into small chunks

415g can refried beans

198g can sweetcorn, rinsed and drained

700ml bottle passata

1 tsp golden caster sugar

10 flour tortilla wraps

2 × 142ml pots soured cream

200g/7oz Cheddar, grated

1 Heat 2 tablespoons of the oil in your largest pan, then fry the onions, peppers, chopped chillies and coriander stalks with half the garlic for 10 minutes until soft. Stir in 2 teaspoons each of the ground coriander and the cumin seeds, then fry for 1 minute more. In another frying pan fry the chicken in the remaining oil, in batches, until browned – add it to the pan of veg as it is done.

2 Stir the beans, sweetcorn, coriander leaves and 150ml of the passata into the veg and chicken. In a bowl, mix the rest of the passata with the remaining garlic and spices and the sugar, then set aside.

3 To assemble, lay the tortillas on a board and divide the chicken mixture among them, folding over the ends and rolling them up to seal. Divide the passata sauce among the dishes you are using, then top with the enchiladas. Dot over the soured cream, sprinkle with grated cheese and scatter with the sliced chilli.

4 Heat oven to 200C/180C fan/gas 6, bake for 30 minutes, then serve.

PER SERVING 490 kcals, protein 35g, carbs 44g, fat 21g, sat fat 9g, fibre 2g, sugar 10g, salt 2.70g

Cheesy broccoli–pasta bake

This recipe is so versatile – use up whatever dried pasta you have in your storecupboard and adapt the sauce to suit your tastes.

TAKES 40 MINUTES ● SERVES 6–8

1 litre/1¾ pints milk
2 garlic cloves, bashed
2 bay leaves
500g/1lb 2oz dried pasta
350g/12oz broccoli, in small florets
75g/2½oz butter
75g/2½oz plain flour
a little freshly grated nutmeg
1 tsp mustard powder
small bunch parsley, roughly chopped
200g/7oz cheese, grated (Cheddar,
    Parmesan, Gruyère, or a mixture)

1 Bring the milk, garlic and bay leaves to the boil in a small pan, then remove from the heat and leave to infuse. Cook the pasta to al dente following the pack instructions (if you're freezing the dish, cook for 1 minute less), adding the broccoli for the final 2 minutes. Drain.

2 Strain the milk into a jug. Heat the butter in the pan until foaming then stir in the flour for 1 minute. Add the milk, a little at a time, stirring or whisking as you go. Bubble for 1–2 minutes, stirring constantly until you have a thick sauce.

3 Remove from the heat and stir in some nutmeg, the mustard powder, parsley, three-quarters of the cheese and some seasoning. Combine with the pasta and broccoli, and transfer to one large heatproof dish or individual ones. Scatter over the remaining cheese and either cool and freeze, or heat the grill to high and cook for 2–3 minutes until golden and bubbling.

PER SERVING 667 kcals, protein 28g, carbs 82g, fat 27g, sat fat 16g, fibre 5g, sugar 11g, salt 0.98g

Sweet & sticky wings with classic slaw

Chicken wings are cheap and make great help-yourself pick-up-and-eat food – just make sure you have plenty of napkins to hand.

TAKES 50 MINUTES • SERVES 6

4 tbsp ketchup
4 garlic cloves, crushed
3 tbsp light brown soft sugar
2 tbsp sweet chilli sauce
4 tbsp dark soy sauce
1kg/2lb 4oz chicken wings

FOR THE SLAW

1 small white cabbage, shredded
3 large carrots, grated
1 large onion, thinly sliced
2 tbsp sweet chilli sauce
8 tbsp light salad cream or mayo

1 Heat oven to 200C/180C fan/gas 6. In a large bowl, mix the ketchup, garlic, sugar, sweet chilli sauce and the soy sauce with some seasoning. Tip in the chicken wings and toss to combine so that they are all coated. Transfer to a large roasting tin or two smaller ones, in a single layer. Roast for 35–40 minutes until cooked through and golden.

2 Meanwhile, make the slaw. Mix the vegetables with the chilli sauce, salad cream or mayo and some seasoning. Pile the wings on to a large platter and transfer the slaw to a serving bowl. Let everyone dig in and help themselves.

PER SERVING 341 kcals, protein 19g, carbs 27g, fat 18g, sat fat 4g, fibre 4g, sugar 25g, salt 2.61g

Jacket potatoes with home-baked beans

These good-for-you beans are great for making ahead and reheating in the microwave – spoon on to granary toast for a superquick supper.

TAKES 1½ HOURS • SERVES 4

4 baking potatoes
1 tbsp sunflower oil
1 carrot, diced
1 celery stalk, diced
400g can haricot beans, drained and rinsed
2 tomatoes, chopped
1 tsp paprika (sweet or hot, depending on taste)
1 tsp Worcestershire sauce
2 tbsp snipped chives, to serve

1 Heat oven to 200C/180C fan/gas 6. Scrub the potatoes and dry well, then prick in several places with a fork. Bake directly on the oven shelf for 1–1½ hours, until they feel soft when squeezed.

2 After 30 minutes, heat the oil in a pan and gently cook the carrot and celery for 10 minutes until softened. Add the beans, tomatoes and paprika, and cook gently for a further 5 minutes until the tomatoes are softened and pulpy. Stir in 100ml.3½fl oz water and the Worcestershire sauce, cook for a further 5 minutes then cover and keep warm.

3 Split open the potatoes and spoon in the beans. Scatter with chives and serve piping hot.

PER SERVING 237 kcals, protein 8g, carbs 45g, fat 4g, sat fat none, fibre 8g, sugar 5g, salt 0.19g

Feed-the-team cheeseburgers

Whether you've got the rest of the team to feed or you're planning a big summer barbecue, a classic cheeseburger will be a surefire hit.

TAKES 35 MINUTES • MAKES 12

1kg/2lb 4oz minced beef
300g/10oz breadcrumbs
140g/5oz extra-mature or mature
  Cheddar, grated
4 tbsp Worcestershire sauce
small bunch flat-leaf parsley, finely
  chopped
2 eggs, beaten

TO SERVE

split burger buns, sliced tomatoes, red
  onion slices, lettuce, tomato
sauce, coleslaw, wedges or fries

1 Crumble the mince into a large bowl, then tip in the breadcrumbs, cheese, Worcestershire sauce, parsley and eggs with 1 teaspoon ground black pepper and 1–2 teaspoons salt. Mix with your hands to combine everything thoroughly. Shape the mix into 12 burgers. Chill for up to 24 hours until ready to cook.

2 To cook the burgers, heat grill to high or fire up a barbecue. Grill or barbecue the burgers for 6–8 minutes on each side until cooked through. Meanwhile, warm as many buns as you need in a foil-covered baking tray below the grilling burgers or toast them on the barbecue. Let everyone assemble their own using their favourite accompaniments.

PER SERVING 343 kcals, protein 24g, carbs 20g, fat 19g, sat fat 9g, fibre 1g, sugar 1g, salt 1.05g

Italian meatloaf

For a fully balanced meal, serve this with jacket potatoes (cooked alongside the meatloaf), green beans and either gravy or tomato sauce.

TAKES 1 HOUR • SERVES 4

50g/2oz fresh white breadcrumbs
4 tbsp finely grated Parmesan
500g pack lean minced beef
1 onion, finely chopped
100g/4oz pancetta, chopped
1 garlic clove, chopped
1 egg, beaten
1 tsp tomato purée
potatoes and green beans

1 Heat oven to 190C/170C fan/gas 5. Line the long sides and base of a 900g loaf tin with double-thickness baking parchment. Mix 2 tablespoons each of the breadcrumbs and Parmesan in a small bowl and set aside. Tip all the remaining ingredients into a large bowl with a good shake of salt and pepper and mix well – hands are the best for this job.

2 Press the mixture into the loaf tin and sprinkle with the reserved crumb mixture. Bake for 40–45 minutes until the top is golden and crunchy. If the top does not colour in the oven, pop the tin under the grill and brown the top for 5 minutes. Cool in the tin for 5 minutes, then lift out using the parchment and put on a board. Slice and serve with potatoes and green beans.

PER SERVING 411 kcals, protein 39g, carbs 13g, fat 23g, sat fat 10g, fibre 1g, sugar 3g, salt 2.01g

Lentil ragù

Struggle to get your five-a-day? This superhealthy ragù will get you four steps closer and can be batch-cooked and frozen for extra convenience.

TAKES 1½ HOURS • SERVES 6

3 tbsp olive oil
2 onions, finely chopped
3 carrots, finely chopped
3 celery sticks, finely chopped
3 garlic cloves, crushed
500g bag dried red split lentils
2 × 400g cans chopped tomatoes
2 tbsp tomato purée
2 tsp each dried oregano and dried thyme
3 bay leaves
2 vegetable stock cubes, made up to 1 litre stock
500g/1lb 2oz spaghetti
Parmesan or vegetarian equivalent, to garnish

1 Heat the oil in a large pan and add the onions, carrots, celery and garlic. Cook gently for 15–20 minutes until everything is softened. Stir in the lentils, chopped tomatoes, tomato purée, herbs and stock. Bring to a simmer, then cook for 40–50 minutes until the lentils are tender and saucy – splash in water, if you need. Season to taste.

2 If eating straight away, keep on a low heat while you cook the spaghetti, following the pack instructions. Drain well, divide among pasta bowls or plates, spoon sauce over the top and grate over some cheese. Alternatively, cool the sauce and chill for up to 3 days. Or freeze for up to 3 months. Simply defrost portions overnight at room temperature, then reheat gently and serve straight away.

PER SERVING 662 kcals, protein 33g, carbs 120g, fat 9g, sat fat 1g, fibre 10g, sugar 14g, salt 1.05g

Baked apples

You can easily change the stuffing – use chopped dried apricots instead of sultanas, and adding flaked almonds or chopped hazelnuts will give it some crunch.

TAKES 45 MINUTES ● **SERVES 6**

6 eating apples
handful sultanas
2 tbsp light muscovado sugar
1 tsp ground cinnamon
matchbox-size piece of butter
2 tsp demerara sugar
yogurt or single cream, to serve
    (optional)

1 Heat oven to 200C/180C fan/gas 6. Sit each apple on the worktop, push the apple corer into the centre of each one then score around the circumference with a small, sharp knife.

2 Mix the sultanas, muscovado sugar and cinnamon together in a bowl. Stand up the apples, side by side, in a baking dish. Using your fingers, push a little bit of the sultana mixture into each apple, using up all the mixture among them. Add a blob of butter to the top of each apple and sprinkle over the demerara sugar. Bake in the oven for 20 minutes or until the apples are cooked through, then served with yogurt or single cream, if you like.

PER SERVING 127 kcals, protein 1g, carbs 25g, fat 4g, sat fat 2g, fibre 2g, sugar 24g, salt 0.07g

Apple–berry crumble

There is no better way to round off a Sunday lunch than with a homely crumble.
Prepare it ahead to make it even easier.

TAKES 1 HOUR • SERVES 6

8 eating apples
1 tsp ground cinnamon
3 tbsp sugar (any kind)
½ orange
punnet raspberries or blackberries
85g/3oz cold butter
50g/2oz plain flour
50g/2oz rolled oats

1 Heat oven to 200C/180C fan/ gas 6. Peel the apples with a potato peeler, quarter them, cut out the cores, then chop up the peeled and cored apple. Tip the apple into a bowl with the cinnamon and 1 tablespoon of the sugar. Squeeze the juice from the halved orange and add to the bowl too. Add the berries to the bowl and mix everything together. Tip the fruit mixture into a baking dish and pat it down.

2 Chop three-quarters of the butter into small pieces. Put it in a bowl with the flour. Use your fingers to pinch and rub the butter into the flour until it resembles breadcrumbs.

3 Stir the oats and the rest of the sugar into the flour mixture, then sprinkle it on top of the apples and berries in the baking dish. Dot the rest of the butter over the crumble. Bake in the oven for 40 minutes or until the apple is cooked. Eat with ice cream or custard.

PER SERVING 260 kcals, protein 3g, carbs 39g, fat 11g, sat fat 7g, fibre 4g, sugar 27g, salt 0.17g

Plum Betty

If you haven't got a food processor in which to make the breadcrumbs, just use shop-bought ones. Make sure they are fresh not dried, though.

TAKES 1 HOUR 10 MINUTES

● **SERVES 8**

200g/7oz wholemeal bread, torn into chunks

85g/3oz butter, melted

85g/3oz demerara sugar

1 tsp ground cinnamon

1.25kg/2lb 12oz plums, quartered and stoned

2 tbsp caster sugar

1 tbsp cornflour

natural yogurt, to serve

1 Heat oven to 200C/180C fan/gas 6. Whizz the bread to chunky crumbs in a food processor. Spread over a large baking sheet and bake for 10–12 minutes, stirring now and then until evenly crisp. Scrape into a bowl and stir in the butter, sugar and cinnamon. Reduce oven to 160C/140C fan/gas 3.

2 Put the plums, sugar and cornflour into a large lidded pan. On the heat, stir for 1–2 minutes until the cornflour is incorporated. Add 200ml/7fl oz water, cover and simmer for 15–20 minutes.

3 Layer up the plums and crumbs in an ovenproof dish, finishing with a layer of crumbs, and bake for 20 minutes. Serve with yogurt to dollop over.

PER SERVING 253 kcals, protein 3g, carbs 41g, fat 10g, sat fat 6g, fibre 4g, sugar 30g, salt 0.28g

Banana & custard tiramisu

This fruity twist on the Italian classic can be made in individual glasses, as here, or in a large bowl like a big trifle.

TAKES 20 MINUTES • SERVES 4

3 tsp instant coffee granules
½ × 250g pot mascarpone
250ml/9fl oz fresh vanilla custard
1 tbsp icing sugar
100g/4oz sponge fingers or trifle
    sponges
2 large bananas, sliced
15g/½oz dark chocolate, grated

1 Put the coffee in a shallow dish and dissolve it in 150ml/¼ pint boiling water. Set out four sundae glasses or teacups. Whisk together the mascarpone, custard and sugar until smooth. Dip a couple of sponge fingers or trifle sponges into the now cooled coffee for a few seconds until soaked but not soggy, then put them into the bottom of one of the glasses, breaking them to fit, if needed. Repeat, using enough fingers to make a decent layer of sponge at the bottom of each glass.

2 Spoon over a layer of the mascarpone custard, then top with some sliced banana and a sprinkling of chocolate. Repeat the layers, ending with a slice or two of banana and a final scattering of chocolate, then chill for 10 minutes before serving.

PER SERVING 398 kcals, protein 5g, carbs 52g, fat 20g, sat fat 13g, fibre 1g, sugar 41g, salt 0.23g

Apple & date turnover

All the flavour and comfort of a fruit pie without using a special pie tin.

TAKES 40 MINUTES ● SERVES 4–6

1 tbsp plain flour, plus extra for rolling
375g pack all-butter puff pastry
2 eating apples, peeled, cored and
   finely chopped
2 pitted dates, finely chopped
25g/1oz caster sugar
½ tsp ground cinnamon
1 tsp lemon juice
1 egg, beaten, for brushing
icing, for drizzling (optional)

1 Heat oven to 200C/180C fan/gas 6. Put a baking sheet in the oven. Lightly flour a work surface and roll the pastry out to a 25 x 30cm rectangle. Mix the apples with the dates, flour, sugar, cinnamon, lemon juice and a pinch of salt. Spoon over one half of the pastry, leaving a border around the edge. Brush the edges of the pastry with a little of the egg, then fold the other half over the top, pressing the edges together to seal well. Slash the top with a knife and brush with the remaining egg.

2 Put in the freezer for 10 minutes to firm up the pastry, then carefully lift on to the hot baking sheet and bake for 20 minutes. Drizzle with icing, if you like, and serve with custard or ice cream.

PER SERVING (4) 467 kcals, protein 8g, carbs 54g, fat 26g, sat fat 16g, fibre 3g, sugar 19g, salt 1g

Bread & butter pudding

Possibly the best and certainly the most irresistible way of using up stale bread.

TAKES 1½ HOURS • SERVES 4

50g/2oz soft butter, plus extra for greasing
12 slices slightly stale white bread, crusts removed
4 tbsp sultanas
1 tsp ground cinnamon
400ml/14fl oz whole milk
100ml/3½fl oz double cream
4 tbsp caster sugar
2 eggs, beaten
½ tsp freshly grated nutmeg
double cream or ice cream, to serve

1 Grease a large ovenproof dish. Butter the bread and cut each slice into four small triangles. Put a layer on the bottom of the dish, then sprinkle over some of the sultanas and cinnamon. Repeat the layers this way until you run out of bread.

2 Put the milk, cream and 3 tablespoons of the sugar in a pan. Gently heat, stirring all the time, until the sugar has dissolved, but don't boil the milk. Whisk in the beaten eggs then, using a sieve, strain the mixture over the bread. Leave to soak for 30 minutes.

3 To cook, heat oven to 160C/140C fan/gas 3 and sprinkle the pudding with the nutmeg and the remaining sugar. Bake for 45 minutes, then turn up the heat to 180C/160C fan/gas 4 and cook for another 15 minutes until the top is crispy and browned. Serve with double cream or ice cream.

PER SERVING 713 kcals, protein 16g, carbs 99g, fat 31g, sat fat 18g, fibre 2g, sugar 35g, salt 1.60g

Cherry–chocolate meringue pots

These quick-to-make smart desserts deliver maximum effect with minimum effort.

TAKES 15 MINUTES • MAKES 4

284ml pot double cream
4 shop-bought meringue nests, roughly
 broken
50g/2oz dark chocolate
8 tbsp cherry compote

1 Whip the cream to soft peaks, then fold in the meringue pieces. Heat the chocolate in the microwave for 30–45 seconds or until melted, stirring halfway through.

2 Spoon 2 tablespoons of the cherry compote into each of four glasses, then top with the meringue mix. Drizzle the melted chocolate on top of each glass and serve.

PER SERVING 504 kcals, protein 3g, carbs 27g, fat 44g, sat fat 25g, fibre 1g, sugar 26g, salt 0.08g

Pears with speedy choc sauce

Tinned pears take all the work out of poaching your own and as a bonus the syrup makes a fantastic base to a chocolate sauce.

TAKES 10 MINUTES • SERVES 4

2 × 410g cans pear halves in syrup
100g/4oz dark chocolate, chopped into
    small chunks
8 scoops vanilla ice cream, to serve
2 tbsp chopped hazelnuts, to decorate

1 Drain the pears over a small pan. Divide among four dessert glasses or bowls. Boil the syrup on a high heat until reduced and thick. Take off the heat and stir in the chocolate until melted.

2 Add two scoops of ice cream to each portion of pears and pour over the hot choc sauce. Top with the chopped nuts.

PER SERVING 354 kcals, protein 4g, carbs 53g, fat 15g, sat fat 8g, fibre 3g, sugar 51g, salt 0.19g

Berry crumble trifles

This pud is great for using up any biscuits or fruit you have to hand. Replace the cream with crème fraîche or some Greek yogurt, if you prefer.

TAKES 10 MINUTES • MAKES 4

2 tbsp good-quality strawberry jam
juice 2 clementines or satsumas
300g/10oz mixed berries
150ml/¼ pint fresh custard
4 tbsp double cream, lightly whipped
8 amaretti biscuits, to sprinkle

1 Mix the jam and citrus juice together in a bowl. Stir in the berries. Divide half the berry mix among four glasses or small bowls. Top with the custard, the rest of the berry mix and finally the cream. Crumble over the biscuits and serve.

PER SERVING 229 kcals, protein 3g, carbs 31g, fat 12g, sat fat 6g, fibre 2g, sugar 22g, salt 0.23g

Eton Mess stacks

The classic Eton Mess uses meringue, which takes about an hour to make. These meringues take seconds to make and then just a few seconds more to cook.

TAKES 20 MINUTES • SERVES 4

1 egg white
350g/12oz icing sugar, plus extra for
    dusting
1 tsp crushed cardamom seeds
a little oil, for greasing
142ml pot double cream
juice of ½ lemon
250g punnet raspberries

1 Lightly whisk the egg white, then stir in the icing sugar and cardamom to make a firm fondant icing. Roll the icing into eight golfball-sized balls (you probably won't need all of it). Two at a time, put the balls at opposite ends of a greased piece of baking paper, then microwave for 30–40 seconds on High until quadrupled in size. Leave to cool for a few minutes, then lift off the paper and repeat until all the balls are cooked.

2 Whip the cream with the lemon juice. Crush half the raspberries, then fold through the cream. To serve, pit a little splodge of raspberry cream on to each plate. Stack a meringue with some more cream, then set another meringue on top. Spoon over more cream, then top with a few whole raspberries. Dust with icing sugar and serve.

PER SERVING 550 kcals, protein 2g, carbs 96g, fat 20g, sat fat 11g, fibre 2g, sugar 94g, salt 0.10g

Fried coconut bananas

This recipe also works a treat with sliced pineapple, and, if you have it, add a splash of rum before the coconut milk.

TAKES 20 MINUTES ● SERVES 2

2 tbsp light brown soft sugar
2 bananas, peeled, halved lengthways,
   then each chunk halved again
150ml/¼ pint coconut milk
coconut ice cream, to serve
toasted, shredded coconut, to decorate

1 Heat the sugar in a small frying pan. When melted, add the bananas and caramelise on each side for 3–4 minutes. Lift out and set aside. Tip the coconut milk into the pan with a pinch of salt, stir into the sugar and bubble until syrupy.
2 Divide between two bowls, top with the caramelised bananas, then add a scoop of ice cream and scatter with the toasted coconut.

PER SERVING 272 kcals, protein 2g, carbs 40g, fat 13g, sat fat 11g, fibre 1g, sugar 38g, salt 0.22g

Fruity fondue

Make more out of fresh fruit by adding a few clever touches.

TAKES 15 MINUTES ● SERVES 4

500g/1lb 2oz mixed fruit, such as
    strawberries, grapes, pineapple,
    mango or melon chunks
100g/4oz milk chocolate
150g pot yogurt (use your favourite
    flavour)

1 Skewer the fruit on to eight wooden sticks. Melt the milk chocolate on Low in the microwave and transfer to a small serving bowl. Serve the kebabs on a platter with the melted chocolate and yogurt for dipping and get everyone to dig in.

PER SERVING 213 kcals, protein 5g, carbs 30g, fat 9g, sat fat 5g, fibre 2g, sugar 30g, salt 0.16g

Hot cross French toast

If you want, for extra decadence, you can also add a layer of chocolate spread to the middle of each sandwich before frying.

TAKES 15 MINUTES • SERVES 4

4 tbsp soft butter
2 tsp ground cinnamon
2 eggs, beaten
100ml/3½fl oz milk
4 hot cross buns, cut in half
a little icing sugar, to dust
vanilla ice cream and maple syrup,
    to serve and drizzle (optional)

1 Mix 3 tablespoons of the butter with half the cinnamon and mash together. Beat together the eggs, milk and remaining cinnamon. Sandwich the two halves of each hot cross bun together with quarter of the cinnamon butter.
2 Dip the buns in the egg mix and leave to soak for a few seconds. Heat the remaining butter in a frying pan until foaming. Cook the hot cross buns for 1–2 minutes each side until light golden – you may need to do this in two batches. Sprinkle with the icing sugar and serve each portion topped with a scoop of ice cream and a drizzle of maple syrup, if you like.

PER SERVING 334 kcals, protein 9g, carbs 33g, fat 20g, sat fat 10g, fibre 1g, sugar 14g, salt 0.44g

Index

Also available from BBC Books and *Good Food*

For 6,000 recipes you can trust see bbcgoodfood.com